THE NEGRO POLITICIAN

THE NEGRO POLITICIAN

His Success and Failure

EDWARD T. CLAYTON

with an introduction by

Martin Luther King, Jr.

Johnson Publishing Company, Inc.
Chicago · 1964

Library of Congress Catalog Number: 62–21536

Printed in the United States of America

DEDICATION

To my late Mother and Father
Izline and Eugene S. Clayton

INTRODUCTION

Nothing could be more important in the life of this nation and determinative of the future of Western civilization than Negro Americans becoming politically aware. This is America's crisis hour, and her Negro citizens seemingly determine her destiny.

These are bold claims, but bold claims and forthright action are the order of the day if the crisis is to be successfully joined.

But let me elaborate and qualify lest these charges be sloughed off as merely the chauvinism of a people only recently awakened to their sense of dignity. The basic facts are that we face a clear choice in the direction which we must pursue as a nation. At this hour there is a moment of anxiety lest America turn its great power and potential to re-create the eighteenth century with its nostalgic rural folkways and simple ethnic patterns. The twentieth century is still frightening and we have lived more than half way through it in fear. The dawning of new nations, new dreams, new demands, new opportunity and new responsibilities amidst an almost unlimited power potential make the best of us quake in our shoes and wish for the "good old days."

This nostalgia which paralyzes America is a grave danger to the future of the world. Amazingly enough it grips even those who have never known the "good old days." As soon as one becomes enough of a member of our society to open a charge account and establish a credit rating, he moves into that glorious middle class and assumes the obligations of protecting the status quo.

History is always determined by the outsiders, the "invisible men" whose collective movements either push or upset the apple cart. The Negro in America has been taken for granted and ignored. Even a Birmingham did not bring any lasting awareness of the problems of this great minority. It took another non-violent demonstration in St. Augustine, Florida to remind the nation of the job yet to be done. Then the Civil Rights Bill presents a huge dose of aspirin to the cancerous racism of the nation. The sheer audacity of the assumption that this was the answer to the "race problem" was enough to provoke a riot atmosphere among those whose difficulties were untouched by the Civil Rights Act of 1964.

And so we face our destiny. Can America remain healthy, morally and spiritually? Can America offer democracy, true democracy, to Latin America, Asia and Africa? These questions are inextricably bound to the question, "can America's Negroes become politically aware?"

The largest block of unregistered voters in the nation are Negroes in Southern states and Northern cities. As they vote, so goes the nation.

This is by no particular virtue of the Negro. It is one of those historic accidents that make many of us affirm the providence of God.

The power of this nation now resides in southern congressmen who remain in power through the disfranchisement of the Negro, and a one-party system. Two million additional Negro votes in the Deep South will change that. This is important because these men not only block progress in race relations but also in foreign affairs, labor relations, urban problems and a host of other important issues.

Northern Negro voters now maintain a balance factor to some extent. But the addition of Negro voters in Indianapolis, Fort Wayne, Columbus, Pittsburgh, Hartford, Oakland, and other "second line" metropolitan areas would give this nation the boost it needs to take creative action on the great economic, political and moral frontiers which now stymie us.

There is, however, a lot more to politics than registered voters. These voters may survive when thrown into the political whirlpool by the sheer power of their instincts, sharpened by years of suffering and betrayal, as did the Mississippi Freedom Democratic Party at the National Democratic Convention, but this course requires too many mistakes and failures. Somehow we must educate a generation of Americans who know the art and craft of politics and pursue it with dedication, integrity and a concern for the progress and future of our civilization.

This book will be an important contribution to educating this new electorate, in whose hands now rest the destiny of the world.

MARTIN LUTHER KING, JR.

CONTENTS

PREFACE

THIS BOOK, *The Negro Politician,* was conceived and written for the layman, the ordinary voter, who dutifully exercises his right to vote, but may not always have an understanding of practical politics. In the past, too many books on politics concerning Negroes have been written for the scholarly in a thesis-like manner that tends to be just out of reach of any understanding by the masses from whom the vote is expected.

This book seeks to overcome that failing. It is written in the everyday newspaper style of a journalist. It places politics, and an understanding of practical politics where Negroes have been concerned, at the homey, neighbor-to-neighbor level within the reach of everyone.

While it deals primarily with the role of the Negro politician in the total scheme of political affairs, it sheds much light on just what that role has meant in local and national elections of the historical past as well as those of the more recent present. It seeks to help the Negro evaluate his importance in the complexities of American government. To others, it will be a source of enlightenment on the significance of the Negroes' roles in present day election and how much more significance this role will take on in the future.

Where there have been failings on the part of Negro politicians, these have been dealt with for what they are — errors of judgment coupled with political trickery. And here the Negro politician does not differ any from his white counterpart. If he happens to be expendable and could be sacrificed to the political advantage of another, then this was and is his misfortune. Not all can be winners in the game of politics, for this is the substance of which the game is made. Unfortunate? Tragic? Yes. But nevertheless true.

If there is any one thing the book, *The Negro Politician*, will convey to the reader, it is perhaps that, despite the seeming complexities of politics, it is basically a relatively simple pursuit. The winner is always the man who has reached enough people — regardless of how he does it.

In almost any undertaking, such as a long and laborious tour of writing a book, the thanks and credit due to the many persons who assist in such a task is immeasurable. I cannot begin to name all such persons who were kind enough to permit me to impose upon their valuable time in interviews or make available to me their personal documents, letters and charts. I can only state here that I am genuinely grateful, and hope that they will accept this notation as an expression of my thanks. I would, however, like to call special attention to John H. Johnson, President of Johnson Publishing Company, Inc. and the Johnson Publishing Company library staff for the assistance they gave me, particularly Mrs. Doris E. Saunders, who encouraged me for several years to write the book and Mrs. Lucille Phinnie and Basil O. Phillips, who gave invaluable aid in all the hours spent in research. Also my heartfelt thanks to Mrs. Ariel Strong who diligently and painstakingly sought to correct whatever errors occurred either of fact, of unintended carelessness and finally, my deepest gratitude to my wife, Xernona, whose patience and understanding enabled me to complete this work.

EDWARD T. CLAYTON

August, 1964
Atlanta, Georgia

THE NEGRO POLITICIAN

Chapter I

THE LOST POLITICAL YEARS

HISTORY has a way of becoming mellow and more romantic when viewed from the distance of passing years. An incident of critical moment nearly a century ago becomes merely another obscure chapter in the archives of yesteryear's records. Yet one such chapter should never be permitted to be forgotten in the hearts and minds of the American Negro. It is that chapter dealing with the nineteenth President of the United States, Rutherford B. Hayes (1876–1880), who in his ambition to ascend to the presidency, was to ultimately cause the political bankruptcy of Negroes for a period that lasted more than a quarter of a century.

Historians have agreed that Hayes ranks "among the worst" Presidents of our country. Many persons possibly have only a vague recollection, if any at all, of him from such information as might have been taught in their high school history classes. No other President in history has permitted such a disastrous bargain to be struck to the utter and complete detriment of the Negro as did Hayes. By removing the Federal troops, which guaranteed their protection, from the South, he brought an end to Reconstruction. For this single act he must and should be remembered as the first major stumbling block in the Negro's struggle for the rights of full citizenship.

The bargain, of course, elevated him to the presidency of the United States by the lowest possible margin of one electoral vote. It was final. It was decisive. It was the all-important majority. It had been given to him in exchange for a promise. Upon it rested the future of the Republican Party, the shaping of American history, and more importantly, the fate of some four and a half million Negroes. If we are to assay the power of politics and the immeasurable importance of a single vote, we must re-examine that power in the light of the period [1868 to 1876] known as Reconstruction.

The costly price that the Negro has had to pay for the vote has been billed, paid for and receipted in the founding of America. Upon the backs of black men, brought in chains to a strange land and kept in bondage for nearly 250 years, America began its rise to economic might. Black men toiled the rich and fertile land of a new America, suffering the inhumanities and indignities of human bondage, to become the backbone of a new industry—cotton. It was their labor, unpaid for though it was, that enabled America to clothe the masses of a ragged world. Cotton production which was scarcely noticeable at nine thousand bales in 1791 became an impressive seventy-nine thousand by 1800 and a soaring half million bales by 1822.

And hand in hand with the demand for more cotton came the demand for more slavery—and more Negroes. By 1831 the cotton crop reached a million bales annually, doubled to two million in 1840, tripled to three million in 1852 and stood at a staggering five million bales in 1860 when the South seceded from the Union.

Unwittingly the white southern planters, in their greed for greater riches, had surrounded themselves with the single force that can spell victory or defeat in politics—numbers. In this case, Negro numbers. Though relegated largely to slave status and considered a thing apart from the body politic, the Negro had swelled to numbers that would eventually make their strength felt in the moulding and re-shaping of a new America.

Of their role in America's physical and industrial expansion, the noted scholar W. E. B. Du Bois wrote in his book, *Black Reconstruction:* "The giant forces of water and of steam were harnessed to do the world's work, and the black workers of America bent at the bottom of a growing pyramid of commerce and industry; and they not only could not be spared, if this new economic organization was to expand, but rather they became the cause of new political demands and alignments, of new dreams of power and visions of empire.

"First of all, their work called for widening stretches of new, rich, black soil—in Florida, in Louisiana, in Mexico; even in Kansas. This land added to cheap labor, and labor easily regulated and distributed, made profits so high that a whole system of culture arose in the South, with a new leisure and social philosophy. Black labor became the foundation stone not only of the Southern social structure, but of Northern manufacture and commerce, of the English factory system, of European commerce, of buying and selling on a world-wide scale; new cities were built on the results of black labor, and a new labor problem, involving all white labor, arose both in Europe and America."

The need for the Negro was clear. When England ceased to export indentured servants to the colonies in 1688, there arose immediately a greater demand for Negro slaves. Where there were only 58,850 in 1715 their number grew to 501,000 in 1775. By the time the first census was taken in the United

States in 1790 there was a Negro slave population of 757,000 in a total United States populace of 3,929,214. At the turn of the nineteenth century there were over one million blacks in America, a population which doubled to two million by 1830, aided in growth by accelerated importations before 1808 and illicit slave smuggling up to 1820. By 1850, Negroes in America numbered 3,638,808, the result primarily of their own reproduction, a probable factor which later accounted for their numerical strength of 4,441,830 at the outset of the Civil War.

To be sure, the vast number of Negroes in America who were to later play a most significant role in the drama of freedom were not all slaves. Neither were they all Africans. Du Bois has indicated that in 1860 "at least ninety per cent were born in the United States, thirteen per cent were visibly of white as well as Negro descent and actually more than one fourth were probably of white, Indian and Negro blood." And more importantly, eleven per cent of this black group were free workers.

That there could be any appreciable participation in politics on the part of Negroes under the system of slavery would seem to be contradiction. For slavery existed in every state other than Massachusetts by 1787. Yet Negroes, as free men, had been voting for at least fifty years before then, and, surprisingly, in colonial times, had been voting in the South in every state except Georgia, South Carolina and Virginia. Even in the latter state they had voted as late as 1723, when it was legislated by the assembly that "no free Negro, mulatto or Indian shall hereafter have any vote at the burgesses or any election whatsoever."

Disfranchisement, the wholesale denial of the ballot to the Negro, became a checkered pattern across America as King Cotton expanded its reign. In South Carolina, Negroes as well as Jews who had been voting, were excluded in 1716. Among the border states Delaware took away the Negro vote in 1792; Maryland did likewise in 1783 and again in 1810. Elsewhere, in Southeastern areas, Louisiana disfranchised Negroes in 1812, Mississippi in 1817, Alabama in 1819, Missouri in 1836, and Texas and Florida in 1845.

The South was not alone in this legislated attempt at white supremacy. In Connecticut, Negroes were disfranchised in 1814. In New Jersey, they were denied the vote in 1807, regained the ballot in 1820, then lost it again in 1847. New York permitted Negroes to vote in the eighteenth century, then disfranchised them, but gave them back the ballot in 1821 with a discriminating property qualification of $250 which did not apply to whites. In Pennsylvania, Negroes voted until 1838 but lost the right when the "reform" convention limited suffrage to whites only.

The Midwestern states, as we know them today, usually did not deny suffrage when they existed as territories, but upon admission to the Union, each in turn, disfranchised Negroes. They followed in this order: Ohio in 1803; Indiana in 1816; Illinois in 1818; Michigan in 1837; Iowa in 1846; Wisconsin in 1848; Minnesota in 1858; and Kansas in 1861.

One can not begin to assess the importance of Negro free men as voters prior to the Civil War, but it is certain that from among their ranks was to come the leadership of the black masses. Consider, for example, Louisiana. There were Negroes here whose fathers had been free when Louisiana was annexed to the United States. In terms of numbers, they had increased from 7,585 in 1810, to 25,505 in 1840, but experienced a sharp decline to 18,647 by 1860 through immigration or, passing over into the white race.

This unusual group played an extraordinary role in the history and development of the state. They organized from their ranks two companies of militia which took part in the Battle of New Orleans in 1815 and were highly commended by Andrew Jackson. They were responsible for many artistic and cultural contributions. One of them, Joseph Abeillard, became an architect and planned many New Orleans buildings before the Civil War. Another, Norbert Rillieux, an engineer and contractor, invented the vacuum pan used in sugar production. While New Orleans periodicals frequently praised him they seldom made mention of his Negro background.

By 1850, Louisiana not only had one Negro architect, but also six physicians, four engineers, and over twenty teachers. Upwards of four-fifths of the free Negroes living in New Orleans could read and write, and there were over a thousand children in school, learning such occupations as carpentry, tailoring, shoemaking, printing, teaching and planting.

This then was the backdrop against which America would have to solve its dilemma of democracy. What status did a free Negro have? What were slaves? Men? Chattel? If they were property how could they be counted as three-fifths of a person in determining how many representatives a state should send to Congress? If they were citizens, then why not equality with citizens?

The answer came with the framing of the Constitution at Philadelphia in 1787. Those fifty-five men assembled in convention to formulate that historic document agreed, at the suggestion of Benjamin Franklin, that for purposes of apportionment the whole number of free citizens should be counted and three fifths of all others. Thus, Article 1, Section 2 of the United States Constitution: "Representatives and direct taxes shall be apportioned among the several states which may be included in this Union according to their respective numbers, which shall be determined by adding to the whole number of free persons, including those bound to servitude for a term of years, and excluding Indians not taxed, three-fifths of all other persons."

From the beginning of America's dreams of democracy slavery was the ever-present thorn that pricked at men's consciences. It was denounced by many, even in the South. Yet it remained, in all its ugliness and human degradation, as the ever-broadening foundation of an economic system that had cotton as its supreme overlord. But it was this very system, forever swelling the bulging money larders of the rich plantation barons, that was to eventually bring a hopeful America to a bloody emancipation. The dreams of vast riches, golden opportunity, and dignity of freedom had made of America a land of opportunity in the eyes of the world. And so the world's immigrants came. They came to escape oppression. They came to seek a higher standard of living. They came hoping to become landowners. And they came in great numbers. By the nineteenth century some nineteen million of them—immigrants from foreign lands—had entered the United States.

Here then was a problem. From among this group was drawn a new class of workers. A class which found itself forced into direct competition for employment with free Negroes and the masses of slaves who had learned to perform many skills. As foreigners they blamed Negroes for the cheap price of labor. The end result was race war, not because of race or color, but because of an economic struggle for bread and meat. A full scale riot, lasting three days, broke out in Cincinnati in 1829 with a mob of whites killing and wounding Negroes and fugitive slaves to such an extent that the majority of the black populace, numbering some two thousand, fled the city in a mass exodus to Canada. Between the years 1828 and 1840 repeated riots plagued Philadelphia, one in 1834 fanned hotly for three days, and caused the destruction of thirty-one homes and two churches, another in 1835, and still another in 1838.

The constant and bitter struggle for economic survival by the masses of white laborers on the one hand pitted against the free Negro, slave laborer, and slave overlord on the other could not help but eventually explode into Civil War. Du Bois has summed it up thusly: ". . . Northern workers were organizing and fighting industrial integration in order to gain higher wages and shorter hours, and more and more they saw economic salvation in the rich land of the West. A Western movement of white workers and pioneers began and was paralleled by a Western movement of planters and black workers in the South. Land and more land became the cry of the Southern political leader, with finally a growing demand for re-opening of the African slave trade. Land, more land, became the cry of the peasant farmer in the North. The two forces met in Kansas, and in Kansas, Civil War began.

"The South was fighting for the protection and expansion of its agrarian feudalism. For the sheer existence of slavery, there must be a continual supply of fertile land, cheaper slaves, and such political power as would give the slave status full legal recognition and protection, and annihilate the free Negro. The Louisiana Purchase had furnished slaves and land, but most of the land was in the Northwest. The foray into Mexico had opened an empire, but the availability of this land was partly spoiled by the loss of California to free labor. This suggested a proposed expansion of slavery toward Kansas, where it involved the South in competition with white labor: a competition which endangered the slave status, encouraged slave revolt, and increased the possibility of fugitive slaves.

"It was a war to determine how far industry in the United States should be carried on under a system where the capitalist owns not only the nation's raw material, not only the land, but also the laborer himself; or whether the laborer was going to maintain his personal freedom, and enforce it by growing political and economic independence based on widespread ownership of land."

Thus Civil War began as a slowly smouldering fire on May 21, 1856 when a group of pro-slavery settlers in Kansas descended upon the free-state headquarters in Lawrence, burning and looting the town, in a demonstration against a newly adopted constitution which forbade the entrance of slaves. In retaliation, the ardent abolitionist John Brown led a small band of eight men to Osawatomie Creek where five of the pro-slavery antagonists were slain. Four years later, with the election of Republican Abraham Lincoln on a platform which refused further land for the expansion of slavery, that smouldering blaze was to burst into a full inferno. A discontented South which had threatened to withdraw from the Union if Lincoln were elected made good that threat. South Carolina called for a convention on December 17, 1860, four days after Lincoln's inauguration, to consider breaking off with the Union, then on December 20, by unanimous vote, passed an Ordinance of Secession, dissolving their ties with the United States. Other Southern states quickly followed: Mississippi on January 9, 1861; Florida on January 10; Alabama on January 11; Georgia on January 19; Louisiana on January 26; and Texas on February 1. Just as quickly they reorganized themselves into a united government, meeting at Montgomery, Alabama on February 4, 1861 with forty-two delegates in convention to establish the Confederate States of America. They adopted a provisional constitution on February 8, then the next day elected former Secretary of War, Jefferson Davis of Mississippi as provisional President.

By April, tensions, reached a cracking point. For three months previous Confederates had been seizing United States arsenals, customs houses and revenue boats in the South. A stand had to be taken at Fort Sumter in South Carolina's Charleston Harbor. The state had demanded surrender of the Union Fort. This refused, the Confederate forces then sought to cut off the fort's supplies and opened fire on the supply boat, *Star of the West,* preventing it from making delivery. The incident was backed up by Confederate General P. G. T. Beauregard's further demands for surrender on April 11, followed by a stubborn refusal by United States General Robert Anderson. Bombardment of the fort began in the grey dawn of the next day at 4:30 A.M. Two days later Fort Sumter fell to the Confederacy with Anderson's surrender.

War, unwanted either by the North or the South, was on. President Lincoln, on April 15, called for seventy-five thousand troops by quotas from the Union States. The Confederate Congress passed an act on April 16 calling for the compulsory military enlistment of all white men between the ages of eighteen and thirty-five for a period of three years, exempting professional and businessmen.

It was, in the beginning, an odd kind of war with an odd kind of ideology. The North did not propose to free the slaves; the South was certain the slaves could be counted upon to remain faithful, dedicated to raising food and money crops for civilians and the Confederate army. It was, after all, a white man's war—a war designed to determine the fate of the Union. In all probability it would be a short, quick fight, then victory, thought both the North and South. The North was counting upon patriotism and Union to rally white labor to the fight. The South, on the other hand, was certain that all white men would rise up to defend the slaveholder's property. The North was hoping that after the South had defended its honor, it would return to the Union with its rights of slavery protected and recognized but limited to further geographic expansion. The South expected to hold onto its secession peaceably, then once victorious and outside the Union, impose terms to insure total recognition of slavery, more cheap slaves, and additional slave territory.

In all thinking, North and South, the Negro was ignored. To the Northern mind the Negro was willingly a slave with neither the will nor the mind to revolt. Southern white thinking discounted any immediate possibility of mass slave insurrection, convinced that the Negro would continue to perform plantation drudgery even in his absence.

Thus dismissed for any military value by both warring factions, the Negro had to play a waiting game. He was a black island in the midst of a battling, angry white sea, and he stood in the center of the tempest, numbering over four million in his ranks, in fact a total of 3,953,740 slaves and 261,918 free Negroes. Despite the fact that nine-tenths of the slave populace could neither read nor write, it is reasonable to assume that they did not need the blessings of either of these rudiments of learning to understand that their yoke of oppression would be lifted merely by fleeing captivity. And flee captivity they did once they realized that the Union armies would not or could not return fugitive slaves, and that victory, once hoped for by their Southern masters, was not at all assured. The Union army then became a haven for the fugitive slave who, fleeing the plantation, sought it as his first place of safety where he could exchange his services for keep and protection.

At first the exodus was a spotty thing, unorganized and cautious. Then, as the war wore on, losing the tin soldier luster of a dress parade and taking on the horrible spectre of slaughter and butchery, the fleeing took on the proportions of a stampede. *The Journal of Negro History* reprinted this account: "On May twenty-sixth, only two days after the one slave appeared before Butler (General Butler, Union commander at Fortress Monroe in Virginia), eight Negroes appeared; on the next day, forty-seven of all ages and both sexes. Each day they continued to come by twenties, thirties and forties until by July 30th the number had reached nine hundred. In a very short while the number ran up into the thousands. The renowned Fortress took the name of the 'freedom fort' to which the blacks came by means of a 'mysterious spiritual telegraph.' "

This exodus, this swarming into the Federal lines, was to serve a manifold purpose in the winning of the war for the North and the eventual freedom of all slaves. As laborers in the Union forces they not only provided the necessary additional manpower to attend the more non-military chores such as cooking, laundering, nursing, planting and harvesting, but at the same time, stripped the South of its much-needed labor force. As spies they furnished valuable information for the Yankee armies, and in time they learned to handle a gun and shoot. They became soldiers, fighting warriors, without legal authority, a loyal and dedicated ally whose willingness and ability to fight was later to decide the war. It is not difficult to imagine that in the hands of some two hundred thousand of these fighting black men each squeeze of the trigger and each slash of the bayonet to destroy the enemy vented his personal vengeance against the outrageous tortures and cruelties of more than two hundred years of bondage.

The role of the Negro soldier became a perplexing dilemma for the Northern authorities and a source of bitter denunciation in the Confederacy. No official sanction had been given their participation by President Lincoln, neither had they received any pay as did regularly enlisted troops. Their existence could not be described with any clear cut policy, and it appeared that the government preferred to ignore them with a "do nothing" attitude. The result was that, within a year after the war began, General David Hunter of South Carolina, faced with the improbable task of holding the entire broken seacoast of South Carolina, Georgia and Florida, took it upon himself to form a Negro regiment. He had appealed in vain to the War Department for reinforcements, but received only repeated replies of: "Get along the best you can." One morning in the spring of 1862 he took the unauthorized responsibility for issuing necessary orders to organize the first South Carolina Infantry, and issued them arms, clothing, equipment and rations. There was no authority for their pay; neither was there any mention of it. Worse, the War Department ignored the action until it was forced to demand information regarding Hunter's Negro troops after a similar demand had been made in a resolution introduced by Charles Anderson Wickliffe of Kentucky and adopted in Congress.

Hunter's reply was a glowing defense of his Negro troops: "No regiment of 'fugitive slaves' has been, or is being organized in his department. There is, however, a fine regiment of loyal persons whose late masters are fugitive rebels.

"The experiment of arming the blacks, so far as I have made it, has been a complete and even marvelous success. They are sober, docile, attentive and enthusiastic; displaying great natural capacities in acquiring the duties of the soldier. They are now eager beyond all things to take to the field and be led into action; and it is the unanimous opinion of the officers who have had charge of them that, in the peculiarities of this climate and country, they will prove invaluable auxiliaries, fully equal to the similar regiments so long and successfully used by the British authorities in the West India Islands.

"In conclusion, I would say, it is my hope—there appearing no possibility of other re-enforcements, owing to the exigencies of the campaign in the Peninsula—to have organized by the end of next fall, and be able to present to the government, from forty-eight to fifty thousand of these hardy and devoted soldiers."

His words of praise, farsighted though they were, fell on the ears of an unresponsive House of Representatives, both Democrat and Republican, who burst into noisy laughter at every word, minimizing his action as an unthinkable joke.

But the war was more than a joke. This war was a gory thing of reality, horrifying in its slaughter, devastating in its destruction. And men had to face reality. The simple fact was that the Negro was a willing and able soldier. He had already demonstrated his eagerness to join the Union forces wherever they appeared, and if rightful military status was to be his, then it must be bestowed by the high authority of those Union Forces.

It was not the intention of the Northern forces to free the Negro and certainly not to make a soldier of him. Yet this issue continued to be the loudest of protests among the abolitionists, and an unanswered moral question in the eyes of the world. The war, after a year and a half of struggle, was costing the staggering sum of two million dollars a day and had taken a toll of eighty thousand men and an expenditure of one billion dollars. President Lincoln, despite insistent urging on the part of some so-called radicals to strike down slavery, waited patiently for stronger public opinion to take hold. It came gradually. The District of Columbia took the first step on April 16, 1862 when Congress abolished slavery with compensation. Then on July 17, the same year, Congress again acted, passing the Confiscation Act which in substance declared all slaves free who should come within the protection of the government, if their owners had rebelled against the government or had given aid or comfort to the rebellion.

For Lincoln the stage was set, the climate was right. On July 22 at a Cabinet meeting he let it be known that he proposed to issue an emancipation edict which would take effect on January 1, 1863 and which would free all slaves. It was decided, however, that in order to forestall any possible reaction to his plan in the fall elections, the document would be pocketed and kept secret until there should be some major decisive Union victory in the field. This, of course, was not known to Lincoln's criticizers who continued to castigate him for moving too slowly. One among them, Horace Greeley, the famous editorial writer of the *New York Tribune,* addressed an open letter to President Lincoln in the edition of August 22, 1862, under the heading: "*The Prayer of Twenty Millions,*" which urged the President to take immediate action to execute the Confiscation Laws.

Lincoln's reply has since become famous: "If there be those who would not save the Union unless they could at the same time save slavery, I do not agree with them. If there be those who would not save the Union unless they could at the same time destroy slavery, I do not agree with them. My paramount object in this struggle is to save the Union and is not either to save or to destroy slavery. If I could save the Union without freeing any slaves, I would do it; and if I would save it by freeing all the slaves, I would also do that. What I do about slavery and the colored race, I do because I believe it would help to save the Union . . ."

Lincoln's dilemma, his resolve to wait for a great Union victory before announcing his emancipation proclamation, came within a month. At sunrise on the morning of September 17, 1862, General George Brinton McClellan, in command of the Union Army of the Potomac, met the Confederate forces of General Robert E. Lee at Antietam Creek, a small stream that empties into the Potomac above Harpers Ferry. The ensuing battle has been described as "the bloodiest day in American history." For hours the two great forces were locked in fiercely savage combat, until at last, as nightfall approached and firing ceased, twenty-three thousand men lay dead or wounded on the field, the fallen divided evenly among both sides. Then as if by agreement, both armies rested for the next twenty-four hours, waited, glaring in silence at each other. McClellan intended to attack again on the next day, but discovered, to his surprise, that Lee had retreated the night before into Virginia, ending his proposed invasion of the North.

Five days later, on September 22, 1862, precisely two months to the day since Lincoln's historic Cabinet meeting and his announcement of emancipation, the President brought forth from secrecy his Emancipation Proclamation and declared that slaves in all states or parts of states that should be in rebellion against the government on January 1, 1863, would forevermore be free. In effect, it gave a hundred days notice to the South as to the future status of the Negro, but more than that it gave new hope and faith to nearly four and a half million blacks who would be willing almost to a man to shed their blood for their new country—their new America. Freedom had come at last. Exit the Negro slave. Enter the Negro soldier. Enter the Negro politician. Enter the Negro man.

The stroke of the pen with which Abraham Lincoln set free America's Negroes might have been the stroke that decided the Civil War. Within five days after the January 1 deadline of the Proclamation, the Secretary of War authorized the Governor of Massachusetts to organize two Negro regiments, the first such regularly constituted Negro military groups of the war. Thus on January 6, 1863, the celebrated Fifty-fourth and Fifty-fifth Negro Regiments of Massachusetts came into existence and the recruiting was completed by May 13. By June Negro troops were in the midst of the fighting. On June 7, at Milliken's Bend in Louisiana, three such Negro regiments had been left behind with a small force of white cavalry to protect the fort while General Ulysses Grant moved the mass of his forces toward the capture of Vicksburg. They were surprised by the Confederates, who beat back the white cavalrymen to the very breastworks of the fort, then rested, hoping to overpower the military installation in the morning. The rebels charged at the pre-dawn hours of 3:00 A.M., descending upon the fort with fixed bayonets, but the Negroes drove them back and held until the gunboats came. In one account of the fierce fighting, an officer is quoted in Williams' *History of the Negro Race in America* as follows: ". . . The rebels drove our force toward the gunboats, taking colored men prisoners and murdering them. This so enraged them that they rallied, and charged the enemy more heroically and desperately than has been recorded during the war. It was a genuine bayonet charge, a hand-to-hand fight, that has never occurred to any extent during this prolonged conflict. Upon both sides men were killed with the butt of muskets. White and black men were lying side by side, pierced by bayonets, and in some instances transfixed to the earth. In one instance, two men, one white and the other black, were found dead, side by side, each having the other's bayonet through his body."

Again in July of 1863 the Negro was to prove his valor in battle. The unseasoned troops of the black Fifty-fourth Massachusetts Regiment were to lead the assault against Fort Wagner in South Carolina, a desperate, almost impossible undertaking, which ended in failure but is a memorable tribute to the black warrior. The following is an account of that grim struggle according to Wilson's *History of the Black Phalanx:*

"Wagner loomed, black, grim and silent. There was no glimmer of light. Nevertheless, in the fort, down below the level of the tide, and under roofs made by huge trunks of trees, lay two thousand Confederate soldiers, hidden. Our troops advanced toward the fort, while our mortars in the rear tossed bombs over their heads. Behind the Fifty-fourth came five regiments from Connecticut, New York, New Hampshire, Pennsylvania and Maine. The Massachusetts went quickly and silently in the night. Then, suddenly, the walls of the fort burst with a blending sheet of vivid light. Shot, shells of iron and bullets crushed through the dense masses of the attacking force. I shall never forget the terrible sound of that awful blast of death which swept down, battered or dead, a thousand of our men. Not a shot had missed its aim. Every bolt of iron and lead tasted of human blood.

"The column wavered and recovered itself. They reached the ditch before the fort. They climbed on the ramparts and swarmed over the walls. It looked as though the fort was captured. Then there came another blinding blaze from concealed guns in the rear of the fort, and the men went down by scores. The rebels rallied, and were re-enforced by thousands of others, who had landed on the beach in the darkness unseen by the fleet. They hurled themselves upon the attacking force. The struggle was terrific. The supporting units hurried up to aid their comrades, but as they raised their ramparts, they fired a volley which struck down many of their own men. Our men rallied again, but were forced back to the edge of the ditch. Colonel Robert Shaw, with scores of his black fighters, went down struggling desperately. Resistance was in vain. The assailants were forced back to the beach, and the rebels drilled their recovered cannons anew on the remaining survivors."

Again and again praise was heaped upon the Negro soldier for his gallantry in shouldering arms for his country, and, lest it be forgotten, his own newly granted freedom. One writer, in May of 1864, wrote in the *New York Herald*: "The conduct of the colored troops, by the way, in the actions of the last few days, is described as superb. An Ohio soldier said to me today, 'I never saw men fight with such desperate gallantry as those Negroes did. They advanced as grim and stern as death, and when within reach of the enemy struck about them with pitiless vigor, that was almost fearful.' Another said to me: 'These Negroes never shrink, nor hold back, no matter what the order. Through scorching heat and pelting storms if the order comes, they march with prompt, ready feet.' Such praise is great praise, and it is deserved."

The value of Negro troops to the Federal cause proved such an overwhelming success that their recruitment was stepped up to such a pace that finally a total of 154 Negro regiments were enlisted. In their number were counted 140 infantry regiments, thirteen artillery regiments, seven cavalry regiments and eleven separate companies and batteries. By official records there were 186,017 Negro troops on the side of the Union, some 123,156 of them still enlisted by July 16, 1865. They participated in no less than 198 battles and suffered losses totaling 68,178. For their heroism on the battlefield the United States government bestowed upon fourteen of them the Congressional Medal of Honor.

In a desperation move, the Confederacy, though at first abhorring the thought of black soldiers in their ranks, finally sought the enlistment of Negroes with the implied promise that service would be rewarded with freedom. The move became official on March 13, 1865, when the Confederate Congress passed an act calling for the enrollment of three hundred thousand slaves, each state to furnish a quota of the total. In part the act stated: ". . . The Congress of the Confederate States of America so enact, that, in order to provide additional forces to repel invasion, maintain the rightful possession of the Confederate States secure their independence and preserve their institutions, the President be, and is, hereby authorized to ask for and accept from the owners of slaves, the services of such number of able-bodied Negro men as he may deem expedient, for and during the war, to perform military service in whatever capacity he may direct . . ."

But the South had waited too long and too late. Recruiting officers in nearly all Southern States hastened to enlist Negro troops, but the Union army, led by General Ulysses Simpson Grant, was descending on Petersburg and Richmond, the Capital of the Confederacy. The end indeed was near. Grant ordered a general assault on Petersburg at dawn on the Sunday morning of April 2, 1865, which was unleashed with such ferocity that long before nightfall the battle was over with hundreds slain on either side and Grant taking twelve thousand prisoners. That same day, Richmond, the once proud Confederate stronghold that had defied the Union forces for four years, was ordered evacuated. President Jefferson Davis quickly called together a meeting of his Cabinet, then packed the records of his Confederate government and fled southward by train. Pandemonium broke loose in the streets of Richmond. Tobacco and cotton warehouses were burned as were the bridges and ships in the harbor. Fire quickly raced through the city and soon some seven hundred buildings were an inferno of flames accompanied with crashing walls and falling debris.

On April 3, Union troops entered the city. The Confederate General, Robert E. Lee, sought to escape with his army, but everywhere he turned there were the Union troops of General Grant. Six days later, with his supplies cut off, his army of nearly thirty-five thousand men in starving condition, and all possible escape routes blocked, General Lee raised the white flag of surrender at Appomattox on April 9, 1865.

The war had reached its closing chapter. In North Carolina, when General Joseph E. Johnston learned that Lee had surrendered he also made plans to cease hostilities and surrender his forces to the Union general, William Tecumseh Sherman. The two met at Durham's Station, North Carolina, on April 26 and surrender was effected with some thirty-seven thousand rebel troops laying down their arms. Within a week General Richard Taylor surrendered all the remaining Confederate troops east of the Mississippi, and finally on May 26, General E. Kirby Smith surrendered the last Confederate army west of the Mississippi and the great war was ended.

For the Union, victory meant the rebirth of a new America. For the Negro, victory meant the fulfillment, whole and complete of his pledged, promised and legislated freedom. But freedom was an intangible thing, not easily understood by the great masses of the four million ex-slaves, ninety-five per cent of whom were illiterate. It is little wonder then that the general thinking among them was that freedom meant complete deliverance from work to earn a living and that the United States government would be obliged to furnish each family with forty acres and a mule to provide them sustenance. Lincoln, in his farsightedness, had anticipated that with the issuance of his Emancipation Proclamation, the time would come eventually when the Negro's status as a free man would have to be clearly defined. He apparently realized that, once war was ended, the emancipated Negro would have to be guaranteed his rights as a citizen. Thus he reasoned that just as the Chief Executive had the pardoning power in the case of an individual, such powers could also be extended to the states. His plan then, made known in December, 1863, even before the Emancipation Proclamation took effect, was a plan of Reconstruction for the rebellious Southern states by which he would offer pardon. There would be exceptions in certain cases, but pardons would be extended in most cases on condition that they take an oath to defend and support the Constitution and the Union, and to abide by the laws and proclamations concerning slavery. It was also his intention that a state could resume its place in the Union when one-tenth of the voters of 1860 in that state had taken the oath of allegiance and had set up a state government.

President Lincoln's plan, however, was not acceptable to Congress which held a distrust of ex-Confederates and a notion that Mr. Lincoln was too lenient in dealing with the insurgent states. Accordingly, Congress rejected the President's proposal, then passed a Reconstruction bill of their own design differing widely from his. This bill directed the President to appoint a provisional governor for each rebellious state, who would, at war's end, take a census of all white male citizens, and if a majority of these would take an oath to support the Federal Constitution, then a convention would be called to organize a state constitution. The constitution should be so framed as to abolish slavery, disclaim the payment of all Confederate debts, and disfranchise the leaders of the rebellion. Further, it must then be submitted to popular vote, and if accepted by a majority within the state, such action would be reported to the President, who in turn would recognize the state government after obtaining consent of Congress.

On the last day of session of the Thirty-eighth Congress, July 4, 1864, this bill was sent to the President for his signature. It failed to become law as Mr. Lincoln, by withholding his signature, permitted it to die by pocket veto. When Congress reassembled in December, there was scarcely any mention of Reconstruction, and it was not until April 11, 1865, the day of the last public speech of Lincoln's life, that the President again brought up the subject before Congress. But he was not to live to see either the end of the war or fulfillment of his plans for Reconstruction. He was felled, shot through the brain, by an assassin's bullet on the night of April 14, 1865, at the Ford Theater in Washington, D.C. The next morning, shortly after 7:00 A.M., Mr. Lincoln succumbed without regaining consciousness. His murderer, actor John Wilkes Booth, escaped but was trapped by a searching party ten days later in a barn at Port Royal, Virginia, where he died from a bullet wound in the neck.

The entire matter of Reconstruction, already a knotty problem for nearly two years, was further complicated by Lincoln's death. His successor, former Vice-President Andrew Johnson, a one-time nearly illiterate Tennessee tailor, scarcely seemed fitted for the great office of the Presidency which had fallen upon him. He foolishly believed that he had the power to restore the rebellious states to the Union with no assistance from Congress, and thus proceeded to act without benefit of that body's sanction. On May 29, 1865, while Congress was adjourned, he issued his famous amnesty proclamation, granting pardon to virtually all of the South with the exception of those leaders of the rebellion specifically identified under thirteen categories, and even those were promised a pardon if they personally sought it. That same day the new President, by a second proclamation, also named a provisional governor in North Carolina whose duties would be to re-establish a state government based on the vote of its white citizens who were to take the oath set forth in the amnesty proclamation. Similar steps were later taken with regard to other southern states, and within two months all but four of the seceded states—Louisiana, Arkansas, Tennessee and Virginia—had established working governments by Johnson's single-handed authority. The four excluded states as mentioned here already had proceeded to set up governments based on Lincoln's "ten per cent" proposal and these were now recognized.

To his delight, Johnson was content to believe that he had accomplished what never before had been attempted in history, that he had succeeded where Lincoln had failed. He had restored the Union, and his joy was immense. Congress, however, took a different view. When its members re-convened in the Thirty-ninth Congress on December 4, 1865, they completely disregarded all that Johnson had done. They elected a speaker, in the House, then considered a motion by Thaddeus Stevens, that a joint committee of House and Senate be named to look into the status of the seceded states. It passed without debate, even while representatives of those states waited outside for admission and were totally ignored in the roll call. Johnson might have brought some semblance of government to the South, but it was still unrecognized by Congress. Yet his action could not altogether be discounted as in vain, for it was largely through his efforts at Reconstruction that a few of the seceded states, though not yet readmitted to Congress, did ratify the Thirteenth Amendment which abolished slavery forever in the United States.

It must be said that Reconstruction, though hoped for and planned for even as early as a year and a half before the end of the Civil War, was not a reality until almost two years after the end of that war. Many months of Congressional debate, led by Thaddeus Stevens in the House, and Charles Sumner in the Senate, would take place before the Union would finally be restored. Both men had an unshakeable faith in Democracy and a sincere belief in the equality of man. Witness then Sumner's speech before the Senate on February 6, 1866: "The freedmen must be protected. To this you are specially pledged by the Proclamation of President Lincoln, which, after declaring him 'free,' promises to maintain this freedom, not for any limited period, but for all time. But this cannot be done so long as you deny him the shield of impartial laws. Let him be heard in court and let him vote. Let these rights be guarded sacredly. Beyond even the shield of impartial laws, he will then have that protection which comes from the consciousness of manhood. Clad in the full panoply of citizenship he will feel at last that he is a man. At present he is only a recent chattel, awaiting your justice to be transmuted into manhood. If you would have him respected in his rights, you must begin by respecting him in your laws. If you would maintain him in his freedom, you must begin by maintaining him in the equal rights of citizenship. . . ."

Such thinking became the embodiment of a second amendment to the Constitution, the historic Fourteenth Amendment, which was passed by Congress on June 14, 1866. It established clearly the Negro's position as a citizen, declaring him on equality with all others in his relationship to the Federal government. It denied any state the right to abridge the privileges of citizens of the United States, to deprive them of life, liberty or property without the due process of law, or deprive any of equal protection under the law. Further, it determined that if any state should deny the franchise to any of its male citizens above the age of twenty-one, its representation in the Lower House of Congress would be reduced accordingly in proportion.

This was the condition upon which the rebellious states were re-admitted to the Union. One among the eleven, Tennessee, immediately accepted the amendment and rejoined the Union. The remaining ten deliberately rejected it. Congress, viewing this action as defiance, took steps toward more drastic measures in dealing with the South. On February 1, 1867, Stevens moved for passage in the House the first of four Reconstruction Acts. This one particularly designed to displace the ten states not yet admitted and divide them into territories of five military districts, into each of which would be sent an army and an officer to replace the civil government. The measure was passed despite President Johnson's veto on March 2, and Congress adjourned two days later, but immediately re-convened in a surprise move to prevent Johnson from not carrying out their wishes. Later in March a second Reconstruction Act was passed which directed the military governor of each district to register all male citizens in the state. Once registered, these were required to take the oath of allegiance, whereupon a constitutional convention would be called for, with delegates elected from Negroes and whites who had taken the oath. The Act further provided that a state constitution should be so drawn as to conform with the National Constitution, and once ratified by a majority vote of the state and approved by Congress, the state would be readmitted, providing its legislature also ratified the Fourteenth Amendment. A second Supplementary Reconstruction Act dealt with instructions to commanders of military districts and the fourth and final measure, dealing with elections, was passed in 1868.

It was thus that Negroes voted *en masse* for the first time in American history. Qualified black voters registered along with qualified white voters in 1867 and when the totals were finally counted, Negroes out-numbered whites by a majority of 43,278. There were, according to Du Bois, 703,459 Negroes registered to vote compared to only 660,181 whites in all of the ten states. In five of these, South Carolina, Alabama, Louisiana, Mississippi and Florida, Negroes were in impressive majorities, and in two of them—South Carolina and Louisiana—they outnumbered whites almost two to one. Yet when delegates were elected from all the southern states to hold constitutional conventions, only in one, South Carolina did Negroes send a majority of representatives with that state electing seventy-six Negro delegates along with forty-eight white.

Within a year and a half after military rule began in the South, seven of the ten states had satisfied the requirements of the Reconstruction Acts and were readmitted to the Union and representation in Congress. Only three—Mississippi, Texas and Virginia—remained holdouts, largely because of the question of participation by ex-Confederates, but by 1870 even these were reinstated. For them, however, there was not only the requirement that they ratify the Fourteenth Amendment, but by now the Fifteenth as well, as it had then been passed in Congress, guaranteeing that no state could deny the vote or the right to hold office to any man because of race, creed, color or previous condition of servitude.

Truly, the dream of Democracy, even though enforced by the glint of military bayonets, had come to America.

The Negro politician now stood erect to write his name in the pages of America's history. For almost three years since 1867 when the Reconstruction Acts were enacted, Negroes had sought elective offices in the high councils of local and state governments and their victories were countless. All over the South they gained such lofty positions as Lieutenant-Governor, Secretary of State, State Auditor, Speaker of the House, Justice of the Supreme Court, State Superintendent of Education and State Senators and Representatives by the hundreds.

Some historians have not dealt kindly with the Negro's sudden and dramatic entrance into America's politics and government, preferring to minimize his political abilities and nullify his efforts as elected officials.

But there had long been Negro free men in the North as well as the South, and from among this group was to be drawn the leadership the masses of blacks now needed. To be sure, many Negroes in local and state offices were duped by the machinations of the plunder bent Carpetbaggers, but there were also those whe served their government with dignity and honor. Notable among them was Louisiana's Pinckney Benton Stewart Pinchback, the son of a white Mississippi planter father and a slave, mixed Indian-Negro mother, who entered politics in 1867 and became successively Customs Inspector, State Senator, State School Board Director, Lieutenant-Governor and finally Governor of the State of Louisiana. He later enjoyed the distinction of being elected a United States Senator to serve a six-year term, after having already been elected congressman. Both seats were contested, however, and after three years of opposition the Senate finally voted against seating him, but paid him $16,666, an amount equal to his two years of senatorial pay plus mileage. One historian has said of the matter: "No fair-minded person can read the proceedings of the two Houses of Congress and the credentials of Mr. Pinchback without concluding that a conspiracy existed to keep him out of both Houses."

Similar excellence in discharge of office is shown in the career of Francis L. Cardoza of Charleston, South Carolina, who served as Secretary of State and later became State Treasurer. Though he aspired to the ministry, Cardoza set out for Glasgow, Scotland at twenty-one years of age with a thousand dollars he had saved from nine years work as a carpenter to get a college education. Notwithstanding the fact that he worked at his trade abroad to help pay the cost of his schooling, he also won a thousand dollar scholarship in a competitive examination among graduates of four colleges, won fifth prize in Latin among two hundred students in his class at Glasgow and a seventh in Greek among a hundred and fifty students. When he finally returned to South Carolina in 1865, he was elected Secretary of State in August, 1868, and served four years. He attempted to resign his post during his first term of office, having been chosen Professor of Latin at Howard University in Washington, D.C. but the governor protested, prevailing upon him to retain his office and appoint a deputy. He consented, accepted the teaching assignment at Howard for the last fourteen months of his office, then returned to South Carolina in 1872 where he was elected State Treasurer in August of that year. During his term of office, he handled between six and seven million dollars in cash and an additional eight million dollars in stocks and bonds. At the expiration of this tenure, his books were carefully examined by a legislative committee and an expert accountant and were reported correct and in order.

These are but two outstanding examples of the kind of leadership Negroes were to provide during the Reconstruction era. It is also interesting to note that the thinking of this leadership was not without logic and wisdom in approaching their new responsibilities. One former South Carolina slave, Beverly Nash, who was a delegate to that state's constitutional convention, has often been quoted by historians for his depth of understanding in remarks made before that group in 1868: "I believe, my friends and fellow citizens, we are not prepared for this suffrage. But we can learn. Give a man tools and let him commence to use them, and in time he will learn a trade. So it is with voting. We may not understand it at the start, but in time we shall learn to do our duty . . .

"It is not our desire to be a discordant element in the community, or to unite the poor against the rich. . . . The white man has the land, the black man has the labor, and labor is worth nothing without capital. We must help to create that capital by restoring confidence, and we can only secure confidence by electing proper men to fill our public offices.

"In these public affairs we must unite with our white fellow-citizens. They tell us that they have been disfranchised, yet we tell the North that we shall never let the halls of Congress be silent until we remove that disability. Can we afford to lose from the councils of state, our first men? Can we spare judges from the bench? Can we put fools or strangers in their position? No, fellow-citizens, no! Gloomy, indeed, would be that day. We want in charge of our interest only our best and ablest men. And then with a strong pull, and a long pull and a pull together, up goes South Carolina."

South Carolina, it seemed, was to lead the way in providing leadership for the restoration of democracy. And this, in spite of criticism and vituperation heaped upon its Negroes by prejudiced newspaper editors and disgruntled whites. One of the most vicious among the latter, one James S. Pike, whom Du Bois describes as "a violent hater of Negroes," did, on one occasion, have a complimentary word to say of Beverly Nash after he became State Senator, but generally he was bitter in his denunciation of Negroes. Of Nash he said: ". . . (he) has more native ability than half the white men in the Senate." But of the entire law-making group he uttered nothing but contempt. Listen!

"The members of the Assembly issued forth from the state house. About three-quarters of the crowd belonged to the African race. They looked like any body of men who might pour out of a market-house or a courthouse at random in any Southern state. Every Negro type and physiognomy was here to be seen, from the genteel serving-man to the rough-hewn customer from the rice or cotton field. Their dress was as varied as their countenances. There was the second-hand, black frock-coat of infirm gentility, glossy and threadbare. There was the stovepipe hat of many ironings and departed styles. There was also to be seen a total disregard of the properties of costume in the coarse and dirty garments of the field.

"The Speaker is black, the clerk is black, the doorkeepers are black, and the little pages are black, the chairman of the Ways and Means is black, and the chaplain is coal black. At some of the desks sit colored men whose types it would be hard to find outside the Congo. . . ."

Despite such caustic and continued objections on the part of some, Negroes, utilizing their great force of numbers, remained steadfast in office on the state level then pressed for participation in the national government. By 1870 the first of an almost unending procession of Congressmen were elected in the persons of Joseph H. Rainey of South Carolina and Jefferson P. Long of Georgia. To Rainey, elected to the Forty-first Congress to fill a vacancy, went the distinction of being the first Negro in history to serve in the House of Representatives. However, it was Long who had the honor of being the first Negro ever to make a speech before the House. Rainey was seated in December, 1870, and although Long was not seated until January 16, 1871, he rose on February 1 to make a short speech of protest against a bill that sought to modify the allegiance oath. It was his only speech—and his last speech—as his term ended on March 4, and Long returned to his tailoring business in Macon, Georgia.

Indeed the most significant Negro political gain of that year 1870 was the election to the United States Senate of Hiram Rhodes Revels. Revels, an African Methodist Episcopal minister from Mississippi, ironically enough, was selected to replace Jefferson Davis, the one-time Mississippi Senator who deserted the Union to become Confederate President. In the eyes of the nation's five million Negroes, Revels had attained the loftiest political post yet, and they immediately began to make great demands upon him for advice and appointments to offices—so much so that he finally had to instruct the doorkeeper not to hand any cards to him during session. His presence in the Senate created such a sensation that within three weeks after he was seated on February 25, 1870, he made his maiden speech and the galleries were thronged to the aisles. Overnight he was to become a celebrity, in much demand for public lectures across the nation. In his brief, one-year term in the Senate, however, there was little to distinguish his presence other than the fact that he was the first and only Negro member. He introduced three minor bills, none of which passed, offered some eighteen petitions seeking relief for politically disabled southerners, and appointed a Negro to West Point who, unfortunately, was unable to pass his exams. When his term expired on March 3, 1871, Revels returned to Mississippi and became the first president of the newly established state school, Alcorn College.

Four years elapsed before another Negro returned to a seat in the Senate, but this one achieved the historical distinction of being the first Negro elected to serve a full term, the first

Negro to serve the longest tenure in office, and the last Negro ever to gain a seat in the United States Senate. Though born a slave, in Prince Edward County, Virginia, Blanche K. Bruce was educated by private tutor on his master's plantation, and after the war took a two-year course at Oberlin College in Ohio. He returned South to Mississippi, arriving at Jackson with seventy-five cents as his sole fortune and a stranger without friends. He was a printer by trade, but became a planter on such a large scale that soon he was independently wealthy. Unlike Revels, Bruce actively campaigned for the Senate, bypassing a nomination for lieutenant-governor in favor of the higher national office. The result was that by the time the Republican party caucused, Bruce with the blessings and backing of Mississippi's Governor Adelbert Ames, received fifty-two votes out of a total of eighty-eight on the second ballot. He was elected on February 3, 1874, and took his seat on March 4, three days after his thirty-third birthday.

As was customary with freshmen senators, when their names were called to be seated it was a common practice for them to be escorted to their seats by their colleagues. This was not to be the case with Bruce. His colleague was Senator J. L. Alcorn, former Mississippi governor, who, as variously reported, either because of a grudge against Governor Ames or resentment of Bruce, did not rise to escort him to his seat. The story of the incident has been told in Bruce's own words: "When I came up to the Senate I knew no one except Senator Alcorn, who was my colleague. When the names of the new senators were called out for them to go up and take the oath, all of the others except myself were escorted by their colleagues. Mr. Alcorn made no motion to escort me, but was buried behind a newspaper, and I concluded I would go it alone. I had gotten about halfway up the aisle when a tall gentleman stepped up to me and said: 'Excuse me, Mr. Bruce, I did not until this moment see that you were without an escort. Permit me. My name is Conkling,' and he linked his arm in mine and we marched up to the desk together. I took the oath and then he escorted me back to my seat. Later in the day, when they were fixing up the committees, he asked me if any one was looking after my interests, and upon my informing him that there was not and that I was myself most ignorant of my rights in the matter, he volunteered to attend to it, and as a result I was placed on some very good committees and shortly afterwards got a chairmanship. I have always felt very kindly toward Mr. Conkling since, and I always shall." [The Conkling whom he referred to, of course, was Senator Roscoe Conkling of New York, for whom Bruce named a son some years later.]

Probably because of his long term of office, Bruce, although at first referred to as "the silent senator" in his early days because he had little to say, did enjoy something of a distinguished career. He managed to secure passage of several of his pensions bills, presided over the Senate on no less than two occasions, and served as chairman of several committees, among them a select committee on Mississippi levees and the Manufactures Committee. When the end finally came to his term in the Senate, he was appointed Register of the United States Treasury on May 23, 1881, by President James A. Garfield, and for four years thereafter his signature appeared on all United States currency.

As has been said earlier, the respective elections in 1870 of Jefferson P. Long of Georgia and Joseph H. Rainey of South Carolina to Congress was the beginning of a great procession of Negroes to the House of Representatives that was to continue for more than thirty years. Before it finally ended in 1901, a total of twenty Negroes had served in that august body as Representatives from eight of the eleven southern states,* (see page 32) with several of them serving two or more terms. They were not wholly ignorant of their duties, as some biased historians have attempted to picture them, neither were they in all cases the most apt among men. It can be said with certainty that at least half of them were men of college training, and that the remainder largely had secondary school education or were self-taught. Only in one instance, that of Benjamin S. Turner of Alabama, is it reported that his education had gone lacking and that "he could write his name and nothing more."

On the other hand, one of them, Robert B. Elliott of South Carolina, is recognized as the most scholarly among Congressmen of that era. Though described as "a fullblooded Negro," Elliott was born in Boston, Massachusetts, of West Indian parents who had settled in the United States. He attended private schools in Boston, grammar schools in Jamaica, then went to England where he attended High Holborn Academy, later graduating from Eton College of the Univer-

*

CONGRESSMEN	*YEARS SERVED*	*STATE*	*BACKGROUND*
Joseph H. Rainey *	1869–1879	S. Carolina	Barber
Jefferson P. Long **	1869–1871	Georgia	Merchant Tailor
Robert C. DeLarge	1871–1873	S. Carolina	Farmer
Robert B. Elliott	1871–1875	S. Carolina	Attorney
Benjamin S. Turner	1871–1873	Alabama	Livery Stable Owner
Josiah T. Walls	1873–1877	Florida	Farmer
Alonzo J. Ransier	1871–1873	S. Carolina	Shipping Clerk
James T. Rapier	1873–1875	Alabama	Cotton Planter
Richard H. Cain	1873–1875 1877–1879	S. Carolina	A.M.E. Bishop & Publisher
John R. Lynch	1873–1877 1881–1883	Mississippi	Attorney & Photographer
Charles E. Nash	1875–1877	Louisiana	Bricklayer
John A. Hyman	1875–1877	N. Carolina	Farmer
Jeremiah Haralson	1875–1877	Alabama	Minister
Robert Smalls	1875–1879 1881–1887	S. Carolina	Steamship Pilot
Thomas E. Miller	1889–1891	S. Carolina	Attorney
George W. Murray	1893–1897	S. Carolina	Teacher
John Mercer Langston	1889–1891	Virginia	Attorney
James E. O'Hara	1885–1887	N. Carolina	Attorney
Henry P. Cheatham	1891–1893	N. Carolina	Teacher
George H. White	1897–1901	N. Carolina	Attorney

* First Negro Congressman elected.
** First Negro Congressman to make a speech.

U. S. SENATORS	*YEARS SERVED*	*STATE*	*BACKGROUND*
Hiram R. Revels	1869–1871	Mississippi	Minister-Teacher
Blanche K. Bruce	1875–1881	Mississippi	Planter

sity of London with high honors. A lawyer by profession, Elliott returned to the United States and settled in Columbia, South Carolina, where he was admitted to the bar, then laid the groundwork for his political career by dividing his time between law practice and the editorship of the *Missionary Record.* From the beginning of Reconstruction and the constitutional conventions, he was a dominant figure in state politics, getting himself elected state representative in 1868, and receiving an appointment from the governor to the post of assistant adjutant-general of the state in 1869. When he was elected to Congress in 1871, he plunged almost immediately into the affairs of that body, speaking out on one occasion in defense of the disfranchisement of southern whites as a "just penalty," and on another for a civil rights bill to enforce the Fourteenth Amendment. His ambition to ascend to the Senate to succeed Hiram Revels ended in defeat and, disappointed at not gaining this high honor, he resigned from Congress in January, 1873. Despite this action, he was again elected for a second term in Congress, this time distinguishing himself with a brilliant plea on behalf of civil rights. It was a stirring two-hour speech delivered on January 6, 1874, in which Elliott reminded his audience of the Negro's patriotism, his participation in America's wars and the blood he had shed in the making of the Republic. When he had finished, proceedings were interrupted for half an hour as other Congressmen crowded around him in an informal congratulatory reception.

Indeed Elliott and all the other Negro gentlemen of Congress who were to come after him earned a place of dignity and honor in the moulding of America, but their hard-won right to participate in this experiment in democracy was soon to be taken from them, abruptly at first, then more slowly, then finally complete removal. Since Lincoln's assassination, two Presidents had followed him in office, Andrew Johnson and Ulysses S. Grant, the latter serving two terms. Now the nation set about the business of electing its nineteenth President in 1876, the outcome of which was calculated to reduce the Negro both financially and politically. In all the years before—or at least since the end of the Civil War and the enactment of Reconstruction—the Negro had managed to uplift himself politically and to some degree economically. It had not been without an unceasing struggle, as the poor whites forever looked upon the Negro as a fierce competitor in the labor market, and the capitalist white planter, once proud and wealthy, but now stripped of all but his land, sought to exploit the black labor that once had been freely his under slavery. Worse, the Negro's political rise, indeed, an almost unthinkable thing in the minds of many whites from the very beginning was never to be without criticism, denunciation, even mass violence. Intimidation, harassment, mob rule and murder were to be the accompaniment of restoration of government, and such organizations as the Ku Klux Klan, organized in Tennessee in 1865, were to launch a reign of terror against Negroes seeking only to enjoy the blessings of freedom. Politics was in a constant state of turmoil, with the white Democratic South hoping to gain strength and control by prying loose from the Negro his traditional Republican vote by reducing that vote to no vote at all.

In 1876, the long-wished-for opportunity that Southern whites had awaited finally came. It was the year of the centennial, a year that marked one hundred years of America's freedom, a year that rounded out sixteen years of continuous Republican domination in government and a year that was to see one of the most disputed presidential elections in American history. The participants were Governor Rutherford B. Hayes of Ohio, whose nomination was the result of a Republican convention stampede on June 14 at Cincinnati, and Governor Samuel J. Tilden of New York who became the Democratic choice two weeks later at their Saint Louis, Missouri, convention. By election day, November 7, 1876, the presidential contest had blossomed into "nip and tuck" political warfare with both sides scheming to claim victory of the White House.

The Democrats, desperate to regain control of the nation and crush the Negro as a political force, would bargain with big business of the North to secure their position. The showdown came on the morning after election day. The nation's newspapers announced the Democratic victory of Tilden, giving him the majorities in such important states as New York, New Jersey, Connecticut and Indiana and all southern states except Louisiana, Florida and South Carolina. He had a popular majority of more than two hundred fifty thousand votes, but he had only a total of 184 electoral votes out of a needed 185, and this without a report of returns from the three southern states of Louisiana, Florida and South Carolina. Hayes, himself, went to bed on election night, resigned to the fact that he had been defeated. But there was still the final counting of the three doubtful southern states to be reckoned with, and upon this would rest the outcome of the election. In all three states military troops were still on hand to insure protection for Democracy and Negroes, and this would constitute the last of such protection in the South. The Hayes forces had promised, if their President were elected, that all Federal troops would be withdrawn from the South and it would be free to superintend its own affairs. Seizing upon such a bargaining position, one of Hayes' political spokesmen, William E. Chandler of New Hampshire, took a hurried trip southward to woo at all costs the decisive votes of those questionable southern states. With skillful maneuvering Chandler was successful in effecting support for Hayes in Florida and South Carolina, but with Louisiana hanging in the balance, the unsettled election became such a disputed matter that it could be settled only by the decision of a high judicial committee. Upon agreement by a vote of both houses of Congress it was finally decided that an Electoral Commission, comprised of five members from the Senate, five from the House and five from the Supreme Court, would settle the election with a decision that could not be appealed. Its members ultimately were to be eight Republicans and seven Democrats, and their votes in all matters would be cast in the same manner—eight against seven. The result was that when their final vote was taken on March 2, 1876, to decide the presidency, their majority of one was in favor of Hayes and he became the nineteenth President of the United States.

The choice, by virtue of the single vote, began a new chapter in American history—one that to this day has continued to deprive the Negro of his full citizenship rights, forced him into second-class economic status, and in many areas denied him his constitutional privilege of voting. True to his promise—or at least the bargain struck by his advisors—President Hayes authorized the removal of the remaining Federal troops in the South, first in South Carolina on April 3, 1877, and finally in Louisiana on April 24. It was the beginning of one-party rule in the South, the open and unchecked midnight terror of the Ku Klux Klan and the gradual political emasculation of the Negro. In every Southern state, through careful manipulation the Negro was pushed back, robbed of his ballot, and relegated to what the white South wanted to be "his place." By law the poll tax became the barrier in some states to take away the Negro vote, in others it was such devices as "grandfather clauses" which stripped him of his rights under the Fourteenth Amendment. The sum total of it all meant that Negroes who wanted jobs to feed their families should not dabble in politics; that Negroes of wealth and affluence who wanted to keep that which they had—or add to it—would by silence and acquiescence refrain from agitating the so-called Negro problem. In simple truth it meant that the Negro, in order to earn a living, was compelled to surrender the political power that had become his by strength of numbers.

The decline and withdrawal of the Negro from the political scene, however, was not immediate, and for some twenty years or more after the end of Reconstruction there continued to be a Negro in Congress, but never in such numbers as they once had been. The last of these, George H. White, of North Carolina, who, in 1897 was to see four years as the lone Negro in Congress, also foresaw the ultimate doom of the Negro politically. Though born a slave, he managed to obtain a college education, graduating from Howard University in 1877, and was licensed to practice law before all courts of North Carolina in 1879. In all matters before Congress he chose to speak, not only as the representative from North Carolina, but in behalf of the nation's entire nine million Negro population. On one occasion, speaking in behalf of a pending tariff bill, White had this to say: "I am here to speak and I do speak as the sole representative on this floor of 9,000,000 of the population of these United States, 90 per cent of whom are laborers. Under this bill they are protected; they are given an opportunity to earn their living. Bread and butter are what we want, not finespun Democratic campaign victory."

White worked unceasingly in the interest of Negro rights, and his final speech before Congress on January 29, 1901, was to be the conclusion of the Negro's most historical reign in American politics. "This, Mr. Chairman," said White, "is perhaps the Negro's temporary farewell to the American Congress; but let me say Phoenix-like he will rise up some day and come again. These parting words are in behalf of an outraged, heart-broken, bruised and bleeding, but God-fearing people, faithful, industrial, loyal people, rising people, full of potential force. . . . The only apology that I have to make for the earnestness with which I have spoken is that I am pleading for the life, the liberty, the future happiness, and manhood suffrage for one-eighth of the entire population of the United States."

His term ended on March 4, 1901, and with it ended the Negro's participation in national government and politics. More than a quarter of a century passed before White's words, prophetic as they were, found fulfillment. Each year moved silently into the next, with the Negro looking on in anxious observance, realizing all the while that as each year slipped past another was added to the silent void of his lost political years. Finally, December 18, 1929, Oscar DePriest, the fearless, white-haired Chicago politician, was elected as Congressman from the First District of Illinois, thus ending the Negro's exile from national political life.

Chapter II

THE KEY TO THE POLITICAL MACHINE

IT has been said that a rose by any other name would smell just as sweet. Not so in politics. If politics could be called by any name other than politics there probably would be countless thousands more seeking public office than there already are. The word itself, though the very system and backbone of Democratic government, somehow never seems to suggest the loftiness of purpose it intends to convey. It is largely misunderstood by the majority of people who, though they exercise their right and are proud to vote, do not know and understand politics. Because of this, the work of the politician is often confined to a selected few, who by chance or design know the rewards of active participation in helping decide who is to run America's cities, counties, states and the nation.

How does one get into the inner circles of these chosen few?

It's simple. Just choose your party and volunteer for work. And you have just become a politician. Your progress may depend upon your assignment, your qualifications to do the job, and your ability to help deliver the vote for your party. But success or failure will depend on you—and the city in which you live. Politics is largely a local matter, and there are hardly any two cities in America where the business of politics is conducted in the same manner. Among Negroes this variation from city to city can either work to facilitate his participation in politics, or to frustrate his efforts entirely. Examples of both extremes would point to Chicago on the one hand, which has developed the most powerful political organization among Negroes to be found anywhere in the world, and Los Angeles on the other hand, which to date has been able to place only two Negroes in elected office.

The reason for the difference lies wholly in the electoral system of each city. Chicago is divided into fifty wards with an average population of about seventy-five thousand, each of which elects an alderman to the city council. Its densely populated Negro South Side elected its first Negro to the city council in 1915, now has a total of seven. By contrast, Los Angeles has divisions of fifteen councilmanic districts, each of which is approximately twice the size of Chicago's wards, and although Negroes number 334,916 or 16.8 per cent of the city's 2,479,015 population, they were unable to elect a Negro to the city council until recently. The reason? The city, by law, redrew its district lines every four years, and it did so in such a manner that placed registered Negro voters in a minority in each district. Many sympathetic whites agreed that this was deliberate gerrymandering, as we shall see later in closer inspection of the Negro and Los Angeles politics.

The vast powerhouse of political power that exists among Negroes in Chicago is the outgrowth of years of skillful and clever maneuvering. Its colorful history, spanning over half a century, is virtually a blueprint for the novice who hopes to get ahead in politics.

The Negro might not always have been in the midst of this riotous drama of politics, but he learned well the complexities of its machinery and put it to good use. He remembered from Reconstruction that numbers meant strength, and strength meant advantage. It made no difference if his numbers were to be counted on the other side of the tracks in the black ghettos of the South, or if they were to be counted along the new tree-lined black ghettos of Chicago's South Side. All that mattered was that they be counted—and that they be solidly counted Negro. This then was the beginning of a new era of Negroes in politics, and one that to this day has withstood the test of time, unmatched anywhere in modern Negro America. Today, this piece of black machinery, this gigantic cog in American politics, has been responsible for deciding who shall be mayor of Chicago, the nation's second largest city, and has held in its hands on no less than two occasions the awful balance of power that has placed two Presidents—Truman and Kennedy—in the coveted seat of the White House. It is a well-organized, tightly controlled mass that today engulfs a concentration of 812,637 Negroes in Chicago who constitute 23.6 per cent of the city's 3,550,404 population. Holding its reins is the nation's most powerful Negro Democrat, seventy-eight-year-old Congressman William Levi Dawson, who has maintained his seat in the House of Representatives continuously for twenty-four years—longer than any Negro before in history. He is the "boss." He is the "kingpin." He is the decision-maker. He is the leader. He is also an old man—a tired old man—who after more than a quarter of a century in the forefront of Negro politics, now ponders his choice of a successor and the future of the organization he practically built from a pattern of his own design. He is at once loved, admired, hated, and feared, but those are the fortunes and misfortunes of politics. And Dawson, the "old man," is a politician of the first order, and a successful one in the truest sense.

If one would aspire to emulate Dawson, to rise step by step up the ladder to political heights, one would have to first heed his advice of beginning at the bottom. The bottom, in this instance, meant invested years of groundwork carefully laid in the midst of the competitive political arena, sidestepping the entrapments of opponents and ducking the lethal volleys of enemies. Few politicians, successful though they may appear, have not at some point or another, experienced a baptism of fire. Dawson is no exception.

What has helped make Dawson successful, however, or for that matter, what has helped make Chicago's Negroes the envy of political achievement, is easily understood in the ghetto-like community of the Negro population and the grass roots, doorbell ringing structure of its politics. It wasn't by design or planning on the part of Negroes. It was a combination of several things: 1) World War I; 2) Negro migration; and 3) the white man's desire to keep the Negro circumscribed in "his community," among his own kind. This, despite the fact that a handsome, French-speaking Negro trader, Jean Baptiste Point de Saible, founded the city somewhere around 1790 by landing at what is now described as the mouth of the Chicago River. He settled at a place, appropriately called "Eschikagou" by the Potawatomi Indian inhabitants, roughly translated to mean "the place of the evil smell."

Until the year 1900, there were barely thirty thousand Negroes in Chicago. In fact, the thirteenth U. S. Census listed the total Negro population as 30,150, of which slightly more than a third or 12,414 were adults. They were relatively unimportant politically, but the picture began to change in 1910. The threat of war, and finally war itself in 1914, was accompanied by an exodus of northern white labor to return to Europe, pick up arms and defend their mother countries. The crux of it all was that cities began to experience a manpower shortage at a time when profit and production were highest. The answer, just as it had been found in turning the tide of the Civil War, was again found in the Negro—the Negro mass of the South.

The Negro came in answer to the call for manpower. He

came at the invitation of northern recruiters who went in search of him in the South, sometimes with pocketsful of one-way railroad tickets North, until at last the South began to impose law after law against their intervention lest they be stripped of their labor pool of Negro workers.

But the Negro came. And he came to Chicago in vast numbers—some fifty thousand of them between the years 1910 and 1920. He came at the beckon of Negro newspaper publisher Robert S. Abbott whose *Chicago Defender* columns enticed, pleaded, challenged, promised and shamed the southern Negro into migrating North with such editorial compulsion that the paper was finally banned in many southern areas. By 1920, when this encouraged migration of Negroes North finally ended, Chicago's Negro population had swelled to over one hundred thousand, a phenomenal growth of 148 per cent in ten years—nearly all of them living compactly in the pregnant, ever-expanding black bowels of a solid South Side.

The Negro had responded to the invitation. He had come North to the demand of labor—and a job to support his family. But he had come so suddenly and so overwhelmingly that by now he was a problem—or at least he was a problem to those whites who had to compete against him for jobs, and the wealthier whites near Lake Michigan's front who had invested in residential property and preferred not to have Negroes for neighbors.

The only welcome mat truly extended him was that of the discerning politician who, with adding machine-like calculation, counted the Negro numbers on one hand, and translated them into vote utility on the other. It was basic politics, and it was ideally suited for the local administrations of the era. The era has sometimes been referred to as the Negro's "Golden Era" in Chicago politics, and in truth it is rightfully named for never before had the Negro up North enjoyed such power of office.

It was the administration of William (Big Bill) Thompson, one of Chicago's most colorful mayors, who courted the South Side with such fervor that he became known as "The Second Lincoln," and appointed so many Negroes to municipal jobs that his opponents referred to City Hall as "Uncle Tom's Cabin." He won his first term as Chicago mayor in 1915, employing the simple political strategy of promising jobs and favors. He also campaigned with a duality of oratory, promising reform to those who wanted reform and beer to the laborers who wanted beer. He had the wisdom to keep promises to his Negro leaders and he rewarded them with well-paying jobs and prominent positions. When he took office in 1915 he appointed two Negroes, Edward H. Wright and Louis B. Anderson, to the important, five-thousand-dollar-a-year posts of assistant corporation counsels in the city law department, and named a third, Bishop Archibald Carey, as an investigator. All three had worked vigorously in getting him elected, but he was criticized for placing Negroes in such prominent offices. His reply to these objections was a straightforward answer in the *Chicago Defender* of September 25, 1915: "I know that in some quarters I have been criticized severely for appointing Negro citizens to positions of honor, trust and dignity. I am glad to take the full responsibility and the honor for making every one of those appointments, and I want to ask my critics to be as manly and to come out in the open light of day with such un-American sentiments.

"My reasons for making such appointments were three-fold: first, because the person appointed was qualified for the position. Second, because in the name of humanity it is my duty to do what I can to elevate rather than degrade any class of American citizens. Third, because I am under obligations to these people for their continued friendship and confidence while I have been in this community."

Because of Chicago's ward system and its precinct structure which is based on neighborhoods and numbers of people it was a certainty that the Negro would use his advantage of racial concentration to gain both appointive and elective office. The precinct, which is the very foundation of the ward, may have between five and seven hundred persons living in a prescribed area. The ward, in turn, may be composed of sixty, seventy or even a hundred or more precincts, each of which will have its own captain who is responsible to the ward committeeman. Here, then, is where the most vigorous political activity takes place since the ward committeeman dispenses the patronage jobs which are the precinct captain's rewards for getting out the vote. How long he may remain a precinct captain depends upon how long he can continue to deliver a winning vote for his party. When he fails to deliver that vote, he loses his job.

This, of course, is the long-established brand of Chicago politics, and it was much to the satisfaction of the precinct captains of Mayor Thompson's era. Their jobs were secure in the mere fact that Negroes, by tradition, were Republican and could be counted upon to remain loyal to the party of Abraham Lincoln which had given them freedom. Thus as the legions of Negro migrants poured into the city, they were quickly sought out and lined up as voters in the Republican camp. In return for their support, Mayor Thompson saw to it that they were given recognition. The same year that he was elected to his first term of office, Oscar DePriest, whom we have mentioned earlier, gained the distinction of becoming the city's first Negro alderman, winning a city council seat in 1915. In a short while other Negro leaders began to emerge as astute politicians, seeking and winning office on city, county and state levels. Among them was Louis B. Anderson, an articulate and shrewd attorney, who received the nomination and was elected in 1917 to the aldermanic post held by DePriest. For sixteen years thereafter he was elected and re-elected to succeed himself in office. In 1918 a second Negro joined Anderson as alderman of the Second Ward. He was Major Robert R. Jackson, who had served three terms in the General Assembly, and also embarked on an aldermanic career that lasted for twenty years. When the city redistricted in 1921 to a fifty-ward plan, Jackson became alderman of the new Third Ward and held the post for ten consecutive terms. In the state legislature the total of Negroes elected to the lower house reached five by 1928, and in the Senate a Negro had been serving since 1924 when Adelbert H. Roberts was elected as the first.

It is interesting to note here that some Chicago Negroes discovered the "key" to the city's politics as early as 1920. In that year Edward H. Wright, with the endorsement of Mayor Thompson, was elected to the all-powerful post of ward committeeman in the Second Ward. As the first Negro in this office, his election meant that Negroes were admitted to the inner councils of the Republican party. He was the party's ward representative who had control over the patronage jobs, the power of nominating certain judges, deciding what representatives would attend party conventions, and who would be the candidate for an aldermanic post. Here the ward reins are held, and without them, even to this day, no politician in Chicago—or any other city under the ward system—can be certain of his political success. It has, in some instances, meant the utter failure of some ambitious politicians, and to others years of continued success.

This then becomes the political battleground and it is in this area that friends of many years suddenly become bitter enemies and the intrigue of politics is carried on.

It would be impossible to enumerate all the instances of just how this much-sought political post has helped shape the course of history for many Chicago Negroes, but attention can be called to several careers where it has played a most vital role. Notable among these are Edward H. Wright, of course, Oscar DePriest, Louis B. Anderson, Congressman William L. Dawson, and State Senator William E. King.

Wright has been described by some authors as "The Iron Master" of his day in politics and indeed he was. He was a big man with a six-foot frame, dark-skinned, pop-eyed and with a face like a bull-frog. His temperament was like that of a bull-dog, rugged and unbending. He spoke slowly when he talked, but his word could be depended upon. When he became ward committeeman in 1920 he had seen over twenty years of political activity since arriving in Chicago in 1884, unknown and broke. He had held a job in the county clerk's office, had been a bookkeeper and railroad incorporation clerk in the Secretary of State's Office in Springfield, the first such clerical post held by a Negro in the state, and finally a county commissioner. In the latter post he began to show how forceful and shrewd he could be. Just after his election he deliberately held up the appropriation for the office of State's Attorney Charles S. Deneen to force him to appoint a Negro as assistant state's attorney. When Deneen learned of it, he is reported to have told Wright: "What's the idea of you holding up the appropriation for my office?" To which Wright replied: "You had an understanding with me that in the event of your election you would appoint Ferdinand L. Barnett assistant state's attorney and you have failed to keep your word. Until that is done I shall continue to prevent the passage of your appropriation." At this, Deneen stormed: "I'll have you to understand I am state's attorney of Cook County and you can't dictate to me." "Yes," said Wright, "and I am county commissioner."

As ward committeeman Wright knew and used the policy of strict discipline and "iron-handed" treatment of those he controlled. One of his contemporaries reports that he kept an index card file on his workers, and that as an election day neared he would call in his precinct captains and tell them: "I'm keeping a record on each man in this election, and I'm paying off on the basis of the way you produce. See to it that you deliver." He was a practical politician in every sense, and just as he used money, positions and favors as rewards for his followers, he was able to gain important jobs and favors from white politicians by threatening or promising the support of his organization, or the lack of it. He employed such tactics to remarkable advantage in 1924 when he masterminded the election of Albert George as municipal judge, a most unusual accomplishment since George had to run on a city-wide ticket. All Wright did was extract a pledge from every Republican ward committeeman that they would support George in return for support of the regular ticket among the Negro wards.

Wright held his committeeman reins tightly for six years, securing for Negroes their first state senator and election of their fourth state representative, but he sealed his own political doom in a factional fight with Mayor Thompson. Thompson had served eight years in his first term of office, 1915–1923, and now sought to be re-elected in 1927. He wanted the support of Wright, but Wright faced the dilemma of owing his allegiance to Governor Len Small, who had placed him in his commerce commissioner's job, and who did not wish to back Thompson. Wright cast his political fortunes with the governor and made an unwise choice. The end result was that his patronage was taken away from him, and he was ousted as ward committeeman in favor of Dan Jackson, who was allotted more than fifty jobs as the new ward boss.

Dan Jackson was no stranger to politics. An astute businessman, he had a college education from Lincoln University in Pennsylvania, and with his brother, Charles, and their father, went into the undertaking business. Dan is credited with bringing more modern undertaking methods to the South Side. Politically, he was not as forceful as Wright, but in the Negro community he was admired for such kindnesses as paying rents and furnishing coal for those families that needed it. Less than a year later, on May 17, 1929, he died and Alderman Louis B. Anderson was named committeeman in his place.

Of the many Negroes who jockeyed for political power in Chicago's black belt, Oscar DePriest alone was perhaps the most controversial, yet was cunning enough to outwit his opponents at the opportune time to win the loftiest offices. By sheer craftiness he managed to maneuver himself into office as the first Negro alderman, then thirteen years later emerged as the first national leader when he became the first Negro congressman from up North. He had been politicking since 1904, and after ten years had learned how to obtain the proper sanction from those who held the power to place him in office. In order to become the first Negro alderman in 1915 he started work many months before the primary, holding meetings and getting endorsements. Late in November, 1914, he had readied an appeal for presentation to Congressman Martin B. Madden, then Second Ward committeeman, which contained the endorsements of thirty-eight precinct captains, ministers of Chicago Baptist churches, ministers of Chicago Methodist churches, women's church clubs, physicians, dentists, pharmacists, the Chicago Colored Barbers' Association, the Hotel Waiter's Association, and party workers. The next month he obtained the backing of the Second Ward Republican Organization, and from then on his election was almost a certainty. There also was an attempt on the part of Louis B. Anderson in January at a mass meeting to get his name on the slate for the aldermanic spot, but DePriest was uncompromising. He declared that he alone had been chosen by the Republican organization, and it was the duty of all voters to support him and abide by the organization's choice. He won the nomination handily, and polled 10,599 votes in the election to win out over three other candidates.

In DePriest's ascent to Congress some years later he employed the same tactics. The opportunity actually began to present itself when Edward H. Wright broke with Mayor Thompson. DePriest seized upon the break and offered himself as an independent Thompson supporter. Upon Thompson's election, DePriest then began a power struggle with Third Ward Committeeman George T. Kersey for control of the organization. He wanted this as reward for his great efforts on behalf of Thompson in the campaign and the sizable contribution he had made. At length he finally persuaded the mayor to name him as dispenser of city patronage, which meant he would replace Kersey as committeeman. One report has it that the move was made so cleverly that even the Third

Ward alderman, Robert R. Jackson, did not know about it. The story has it that he went to see Mayor Thompson about patronage in the Third Ward, and the mayor's answer was simply: "Have you seen Oscar?" As an appeasement for Kersey he was given a job under the board of local improvements. But the political plum he had lost, that of the committeemanship, was of greater importance than he realized for the very next year it proved to be DePriest's stepping stone to Congress.

The turn of events centered around the death of Congressman Martin B. Madden, representative from the First Congressional District of Illinois from 1904 until the time of his death shortly after the 1928 primary. A Negro candidate usually ran against Madden for the Congressional post, but in this same 1928 primary in which he was again victorious his opponent was an attorney by the name of William Levi Dawson. Though losing, Dawson polled twenty-nine per cent of the vote to cause quite a stir among the Republican organization leaders. Moreover, had he been a ward committeeman at the time of Madden's death, he might have realized sooner his ambition of going to Congress. But he was not. And the power to fill the vacancy was in the hands of the Congressional District Committee, a five-man group, which included Ward Committeeman Oscar DePriest. They were all members of the Thompson faction of the Republican party. Mayor Thompson was in position to virtually dictate the nomination. All DePriest had to do was act.

As it happened, both DePriest and Alderman Louis B. Anderson were out of the city at a summer resort when the news of Madden's death was flashed over the wires. DePriest acted quickly and *first*. He sent wires to the other ward committeeman, who along with himself, made up the committee that had the power to fill the vacancy. They were: Dan Jackson, Daniel Serritella, John (Dingbat) Oberta, and W. S. Finucane. DePriest told all of them he would like their support for the nomination. Next he sent a wire to Mayor Thompson telling him also of his wishes. When he returned to the city, the mayor told him: "You know, Oscar, I'm for you." Later, when Committeeman Dan Jackson was asked by the mayor if he wanted Anderson or Adelbert Roberts of the Second Ward to have the nomination, Jackson said: "I'm with you, Mr. Mayor." To which the mayor replied: "Well, I'm with Oscar." Thus DePriest had secured the nomination before others knew what was going on as he and Dan Jackson controlled the largest wards in the district.

In the rough and tumble tradition of Chicago politics, DePriest truly distinguished himself. But his struggle to gain office and hold it was by no means easy.

In the midst of the political battleground, DePriest was a man who could stand tall. He never knew defeat, and this perhaps is the secret of his success. Under no circumstances did he ever allow his organizational forces to disintegrate, nor did he allow himself to become inactive or off the scene as a challenge to his opposition. It is little wonder then that this legendary pioneer in Chicago politics, who had been born in a Florence, Alabama cabin on March 9, 1871, would rise up one day to his huge six-foot height in the great halls of Congress, and there, with his massive shock of white hair waving, fulfill the prophecy of George H. White uttered twenty-eight years before:

"This, Mr. Chairman, is perhaps the Negro's temporary farewell to the American Congress: but let me say Phoenix-like he will rise up some day and come again. . . ."

Chapter III

THE MAKING AND BREAKING OF POLITICIANS

THE game of politics in its most practical application is basically not a game for the timid. Neither is it a game for the weak. Among Negro politicians, as among all other politicians, it is a game to be enjoyed by the strong, the alert and the shrewd. It is at best a game of cunning and skill; at worst a cold, ruthless business where mistakes are disastrous. Those who are willing to venture into it seldom are aware of its perils, and those who do not always exercise political wisdom find abrupt ends to their careers.

As we have pointed out earlier, Oscar DePriest was a politician who knew how to maneuver in dangerous political waters. His entrance into Chicago politics was the result of the same sort of maneuvering that was to characterize his career. His version of the story was thus: "A friend of mine came by one evening and said, 'Come go to a meeting with me.' I had nothing to do so I went. It was a precinct meeting and they were electing precinct captains. The vote was 20–20 for rival candidates and I saw right away a deal could be made. So I went to one of the candidates and said, 'Now you're the man who ought to be captain, I'll give you two additional votes if you'll make me a secretary.' The man refused. I went to his rival and made the same proposition. He accepted. I was made secretary."

Significantly, it must be mentioned here that the year 1932 marked a turning of the political tide across the nation. It was the year that President Franklin D. Roosevelt first swept into office in the midst of a great national depression that found Negroes hardest hit. On Chicago's South Side the tide had already begun to turn the year before when the Democratic candidate for mayor, Anton J. Cermak, won out over Mayor William Hale (Big Bill) Thompson in the 1931 mayoralty race. And most importantly, he had won without the support of the Negro community, which again had remained loyal to Mayor Thompson. Cermak had received his lowest votes in the Negro wards, and since they had played no important part in his victory, he was under no obligation to reward them. The result was that many Negroes in important positions and large numbers of those in temporary civil service jobs were dismissed.

In 1932, the year of the presidential election, the Chicago Negro still refused to be shaken in his loyalty to the Republican party. He gave Roosevelt only twenty-three per cent of his vote, but managed to return Oscar DePriest to Congress for a third term in the November election by a vote of 33,069 to 25,303 for his white Democratic opponent, Harry Baker. There were some who immediately grasped the significance of this pendulum swinging toward the Democrats, but by and large the power of the Negro Second and Third Ward organizations was almost ineffectual as it was being counted on the wrong side of the ledger. Thus faced with patronage loss and lack of immediate Democratic leadership, the Negro Republican ward machines began to deteriorate. It was not so easy to build up similar Democratic machines, although an effort in this direction was being attempted by an ex-bellboy named Edward M. (Mike) Sneed, who had won the Democratic Third Ward Committeemanship in 1932. As always, the offers of jobs and favors were inducements to get Negro voters to desert their old party for the new.

Against this Democratic onslaught, Dawson managed to hold on to his aldermanic post for three successive terms, until 1938 when he broke altogether with the Republican party and joined the Democrats. DePriest did not fare so well. In 1934 he had to face for the first time a Negro Democrat as an opponent for his seat in Congress. The opponent was Arthur W. Mitchell, a virtual novice in Chicago politics, who had just come to Chicago in 1928 as a young lawyer from Washington, D.C. Like other Negroes he allied himself with the Republican party, but switched to the Democrats in 1932 and participated in the national campaign. In the Democratic primary of 1934 he sought the nomination for Congress against white Democrat Harry Baker, whom DePriest had defeated in 1928, but lost by a narrow margin. When Baker died shortly after the primary, Mitchell got the nod to oppose Dawson with the blessings of the famous first ward boss Mike (Hinky Dinky) Kenna and the Second Ward Committeeman Joseph Tittinger, both white. Although a newcomer and scarcely considered a threat, Mitchell got the solid support of white Democrats as well as some Negro Democrats to defeat DePriest in what was considered a national upset. The final vote was Mitchell, 27,963; DePriest, 24,820. The Mitchell victory now meant that Democrats in the North had given national recognition to the Negro within their party and that the Democratic caucus in the House of Representatives would now be forced to admit a Negro. It also meant the political end for DePriest who was never able to make an effective comeback, as Mitchell successfully returned to Congress for three consecutive terms.

The rise of the Democratic party and its ultimate wooing of Negroes inevitably presented an attraction for Dawson, who, although he had maintained his aldermanic seat for six years, was still without the patronage and the power of the ward committeemanship he so earnestly desired. During his tenure of office Mayor Cermak was slain in Florida by an assassin's bullet intended for President Roosevelt, and Mayor Edward J. Kelly was sworn into office in 1933 to replace him. Kelly outdid Mayor Thompson in his efforts to win over Negroes to the Democratic party. He not only named Negroes to posts that Thompson had given them, but placed them in new roles as well, naming one Negro to the school board, elevating one policeman to a captaincy, and giving another Negro the chairmanship of the Chicago Housing Authority. He also succeeded in getting a Negro placed on the Democratic ticket and elected as judge of the municipal court.*

Dawson was impressed. He was also impressed with Roosevelt and what he had done for Negroes with the Works Progress Administration. Although still Republican, he became close to Democratic Mayor Kelly, and at last embraced the Democratic party completely in 1938 when it appeared that he might be able to gain a ward committeemanship. On the political horizon at the time was a young attorney, Earl B. Dickerson, who had plunged headlong into politics in 1928 as a Democrat in the national campaign of presidential candidate Alfred E. Smith. In that campaign he worked as Regional Director for Negroes, covering the five states of Illinois, Ohio, Indiana, West Virginia and Michigan. Although Smith lost, Dickerson distinguished himself as a promising young politician. He had served as an assistant corporation counsel from 1923 to 1927, and in 1933 was elected assistant attorney general for the state of Illinois. He was also a friend to Daw-

* Names in footnote or appendix.

son with whom he had served in World War II as a soldier in the 365th Infantry in France.

The primary of 1939 found Dickerson as the endorsed Democratic candidate for the Second Ward aldermanic post held by Dawson. The contest was a heated one with Dawson also facing William King for the Republican nomination. When the results were tallied after the voters had gone to the polls on that rainy Tuesday of February 28, 1939, Dickerson won the Democratic nomination handily, polling 9,241 votes against 1,597 for Corneal Davis, who had been sponsored by factional interests. On the Republican side, Dawson was unseated by King who received 9,217 votes to 8,573 for Dawson, and opposed Dickerson in the general election scheduled for April. Dawson's defeat, however, was not to be passed over lightly. In a surprise move, he switched his allegiance from the Republican party to open endorsement of Dickerson for the councilmanic seat and pledged support for the re-election of Mayor Kelly. He called together his forces in a closed meeting on Sunday, March 19, and delivered a rousing address before more than two hundred precinct workers in which he pleaded for new leadership for the Second Ward. At the end of his address he introduced a resolution and had it passed that his organization was one hundred per cent behind the candidacy of Mayor Edward J. Kelly for mayor and Earl B. Dickerson for alderman. "I want Kelly elected," Dawson told the gathering, "because Mayor Kelly has always been fair to my people. I want Dickerson elected because Dickerson represents the best thought of the people of the Second Ward and is capable by training and experience of making the most outstanding alderman in the city council. He will be a credit to his people, his community and his country." The general election of Tuesday, April 4, 1939, proved that Dawson had placed his support behind a winning candidate. Dickerson was the winner with a total of 19,287 votes against 16,917 for King.

Two years later in 1942, Dawson named himself to run for

Congress, although he first had to face a primary contest against Dickerson. Dawson piled up almost a three to one majority, polling 13,789 votes to 4,187 for Dickerson. In that same primary election his long-time political opponent, William E. King, won the Republican nomination for the congressional seat in the First District, defeating Attorney Bindley Cyrus by a vote of 9,032 to 1,157. Thus it was Dawson against King in the November election of 1942, with Dawson this time emerging the victor on the Democratic ticket by a vote of 26,593 to 23,628. He had at last accomplished under the Democratic banner what he had failed to do on two previous attempts as a Republican and it was the beginning of an unbroken succession of re-election to office with Dawson neither relinquishing his seat in Congress nor the Second Ward committeemanship he had strived so hard to obtain.

The struggle to stay atop the political pinnacle is a constant one in the lives of Negro politicians, beginning almost from the day they start work within the party as doorbell ringers and sometimes ending abruptly in complete political exile. One very extraordinary example is that of former New York Borough President Hulan Jack who invested twenty years of his lifetime in making a success of his career in politics, only to have it shattered because he unwittingly allowed a contractor to pay for the re-decorating of the apartment in which he and his family lived.

Jack's career had been in the typical Horatio Alger tradition. He had come to New York in 1923 as a youth of seventeen, an immigrant from St. Lucia, British West Indies, where his father, Ratford Edwin Jack, had been a bishop of the African Orthodox Church. He got a job cutting paper boxes in the Peerless Paper Box Company, where thirty years later he became a vice-president. He enrolled in night school to improve his education, and after graduation went to New York University where he majored in business administration and became interested in politics. By 1931, as a young man of twenty-five, he was already on his way in the midst of politics, pounding pavements and ringing doorbells to get out the vote for candidates he favored. His first election to public office came in 1940 when he was chosen on the Democratic ticket to run for the state assembly in the Seventeenth District in lower Harlem. He won easily with little opposition and was elected six times to the assembly post and served a total of thirteen years, during which he pushed through scores of bills, two of them designed to eliminate discrimination in housing and liability insurance.

A strong organization man, Jack was favored as the Democratic choice to seek the Manhattan borough presidency. The Republicans already had designated Negro educator Elmer A. Carter as their candidate for the post, so Tammany, in an eleventh-hour switch, gave the nod to Jack instead of their white candidate, Assemblyman Herman A. Katz, who already had been selected to run. It meant that an all-Negro slate would make a contest for the twenty-five-thousand-dollar-a-year office, regarded by many as the highest and most powerful political position ever held by a Negro in America. Besides Jack and Carter, the other contestants were the Reverend James Robinson, a Presbyterian minister and pastor of the Church of the Master, who was supported by the Liberals; Colonel Chauncey W. Hooper, deputy city controller and National Guard officer, who was offered by the Mayor Vincent Impellitteri faction; and Arthur Braun, a candidate for the left-wing American Labor Party. Once the primaries were hurdled, Jack scored an easy victory in the November elections, polling 214,302 votes to win over Carter, who had a total of 135,429, and Robinson, who received 87,293 votes as an Independent.

His election meant that a Negro would preside for the first time over the Island of Manhattan, the wealthiest and most densely populated political sub-division in the world. It, along with the other four boroughs of the Bronx, Brooklyn, Queens and Richmond make up what is New York City, but of the five only Manhattan, that storied Island of 31.2 square miles, presents the facade that is the great and grand image of New York. It alone has a population bigger than that of at least five other major American cities, including Detroit, San Francisco, Cleveland, Baltimore and Atlanta. In it are located New York's Chinatown and that populous area known as Harlem, which is the largest population concentration of Negroes to be found anywhere in the world. It is in Manhattan that Wall Street and the Stock Exchange are located, the Empire State Building, Carnegie Hall, Madison Square Garden, the United Nations, and such famous hotels as the Waldorf-Astoria. It is the financial center of the world, and the theatrical and cultural center of the United States. It pays more federal taxes than many states of the Union, and receives and contributes the lion's share of New York's $1,600,000,000 budget—an enormous sum second only to the budget of the federal government.

As president of Manhattan borough, Jack received twenty-five thousand dollars a year, a higher income than that of a United States Congressman who is paid twenty-two thousand five hundred dollars a year. He was the chief administrator for more than two million people, supervised the spending of a budget of over five million dollars, and controlled some 1,415 jobs in his office, some of which paid as high as fifteen thousand dollars a year. When he took office, his election was viewed as a spectacular political achievement throughout the world and some sixty correspondents covered the event, including those from newspapers in India, Africa, Australia, Germany, Greece and other distant lands. The new post also placed him as the first Negro to sit on the all-powerful, decision-making Board of Estimate, which has the responsibility of spending New York City's tremendous budget. Jack, as Manhattan borough president, had two votes in this body, as did the Brooklyn borough president, while presidents of the three remaining boroughs had only one vote each. His specific duties placed him directly in charge of more than five hundred miles of streets, sewers, building lines, the issuance of permits, and the naming of the members of the city's fourteen school boards. It was under his administration that New York launched one of its biggest public works projects, a twenty-nine-million-dollar extension of the Harlem River Drive, as well as a seven-million-dollar elevated highway which was begun shortly after he took office and completed during the freshman months of his first term.

As an elected official and the highest paid Negro in political office, Jack carried out the duties of his office with as much vigor and efficiency as any of his predecessors. His first four-year term settled comfortably into dignified routine, with few objections to his management of the high office. He had brought with him to the position a reputation for honesty and integrity, virtues which had been repeatedly stressed throughout the campaign. When he received the backing and endorsement of New York Congressman Adam Clayton Powell, the veteran Powell, among other complimentary things, said: "He is experienced. Through all the fourteen years not a finger can be pointed at him because he has been morally honest and incorruptible."

Jack's troubles did not begin until his second term of office. There had been rumblings prior to the 1957 election that he might face some difficulty in his bid for re-election because of a Republican-sponsored white opponent, but Jack coasted easily into his second term, winning by a vote of 292,316 to 216,843 for his white Republican foe, Melvin Krulewitch. However, Jack found himself in serious trouble in December of 1959.

Removed from office, Jack sought to clear his name and at the same time remain active politically. He was successful in retaining his post as Democratic district leader of the Fourteenth Assembly District, a political office he still holds, but so far has not been able to remove the conviction which cost him the Manhattan borough presidency. Jack still lives with his family in the much-publicized apartment that led to his downfall, and whether or not he will seek further appeal in a higher court is a question that only the future can decide.

Politics, of course, went on in a "business as usual manner" despite Jack's loss of office. Within two weeks after he vacated the office of borough presidency there was a brisk scramble for the position with the keenest of behind-the-scenes maneuvering. In a power struggle between New York Mayor Robert Wagner and Tammany boss Carmine DeSapio, who had been feuding for control of the Democratic organization. The vote to fill the vacancy was in the hands of Manhattan's six-man city council, among whom was its lone Negro member, Earl Brown. Brown was a front runner for the office, with the backing of the United Leadership Team, an organization put together by Congressman Adam Clayton Powell and his chief lieutenant J. Raymond Jones. He was ruled ineligible, however, under the city charter which prevents a council member for being eligible for a post the council itself fills. The Tammany forces then gave their endorsement to one of their Negro leaders, Eleventh District Assemblyman Lloyd E. Dickens, who seemed a cinch to be named Jack's successor, until Mayor Wagner, in an eleventh-hour decision, announced that he favored Justice Edward R. Dudley of Domestic Relations Court. It was a triumph of astute strategy for the mayor, whose own political prestige was on the wane at the time and might have worsened had he not been able to effect the election of Dudley by a four-to-two vote. The mayor simply outfoxed his Tammany foes by masquerading as a beaten man who already foresaw defeat, but secretly was busy collecting the necessary votes for Dudley, whom he had named to his judgeship in 1955 and whom he now named for the borough post on election eve. He succeeded in maneuvering away from the Tammany fold two of their almost certain votes—that of Earl Brown and Councilman Daniel S. Weiss, then won over the vote of the council's lone Republican, Stanley Isaacs, himself a former Manhattan borough president. When the vote was cast four-to-two in favor of Dudley on January 31 in City Hall it marked the biggest political coup to be accomplished by Mayor Wagner and a damaging blow to the power and prestige of Carmine DeSapio and Tammany Hall. His candidate, Justice Dudley, was sworn in ninety minutes after the City Hall election, and in his new role of borough president, brought to the office a background rich in political experience. Besides having served on the Domestic Relations bench for six years, he formerly had been President Truman's ambassador to Liberia from 1948 to 1953. He was, from 1945 to 1947, legal counsel to the governor of the Virgin Islands, and from 1952 to 1955 was an assistant attorney general in New York. By odd coincidence, his uncle, Edward A. Johnson, the first Negro elected to New York's state assembly in 1917, served in that body with Mayor Wagner's father, Robert F. Wagner, Sr. Now these two, the nephew and the son, presided over America's largest city, and its largest component, Manhattan Island.

Some attention must be given here to the cruel effects of racial prejudice in contributing directly to the downfall of the Negro politician, notwithstanding his excellence in performance of duties or his superior qualifications. A flagrant example is that of Cincinnati, Ohio, and its former vice-mayor, Negro attorney Theodore Berry. By comparison with other cities, Cincinnati normally conducted its politics cleanly, and while it was not necessarily held up as a shining example of a city with the best Negro-white relations in the North, it did have a fairly decent reputation in its dealings with its Negro citizenry, dating back even to the days of slavery and the underground railroad. It was not surprising then when Theodore Berry was elected in 1949 as the first Negro member of the nine-man city council. He had attempted to gain the post two years previously, running as an Independent to help bolster the vote to save Proportional Representation, the city's electoral system by which minority parties receive representation in legislative bodies in proportion to their popular vote. Such a system had been established in Cincinnati in 1925 when the form of government was changed to that of City Manager. Berry, in 1949, was supported on the ticket by the City Charter Committee, popularly known as the Charterite Party, a fusion of Democrats and Independent Republicans. His victory was the beginning of a career in the city council that found him re-elected to four successive terms and finally named the city's vice-mayor. Under the system it was customary for the majority party to name the person receiving the highest number of votes as mayor of the city, but this was not the case with Berry. In 1953 and in 1955 he scored his biggest triumphs, leading all other Charterites in receiving the largest number of votes, but he was passed over for the mayor's post on both occasions. In 1953 he deferred in favor of councilman Eddie Waldvogel, a Charterite with sixteen years seniority in the council, who announced at the first Charterite caucus: "I am announcing that I want to be mayor of Cincinnati and I will not yield to anybody." He got his wish, but died a few months later. In 1955 when the Charterites again won a majority with Berry polling the highest vote, the mayor's post was given to Charles P. Taft, the younger brother of the one-time United States Senator Robert A. Taft, a Republican stalwart whose ambitions were in the direction of the United States presidency. Berry, in that year, was content to accept the honorary office of vice-mayor, a historical appointment for Cincinnati Negroes, but not what he deserved as the leading vote-getter for his party. He had indeed proved that he was capable and qualified in matters of the city council. Since 1953 he had served as chairman of the Finance Committee and, in that same year, had tackled and solved a six-and-one-half-million-dollar deficit that had to be worked out in thirty days. He was publicized as "the ablest man in the council," and during his tenure of office became chairman of the Housing and Urban Renewal Committee, chairman of the Capital Improvements Committee, vice-chairman of the Law Committee and a member of the Highways Committee. These duties were in addition to his chairmanship of the important Finance Committee which had administered an annual budget of thirty-two million dollars. In December of 1955 Berry was temporarily elevated to the mayor's office when it became necessary for Mayor Taft to be absent from the city. With discreet humility Berry refused to be photographed in the mayor's office on that day of December 15, instead posed for photographers and conducted interviews in his own office. "I will not pose a situation today, pretending there is something to be done, when in fact there is nothing," he told newsmen who hoped to get pictures of him in the mayor's chair. He then pointed out that the city manager was the chief executive of the city and that the mayor is only a ceremonial head and presiding officer of the city council. "On this first day," Berry explained, "I'm advised by the mayor's secretary that there is no ceremonial function to be performed. In the absence of a session of council or a ceremonial function, there is nothing for me, as vice-mayor to do." What Berry meant was that the mayor's office, unlike that of many other cities, was a nominal office with the prescribed function of serving as official host for the city, greeting foreign dignitaries and being available for ribbon cuttings and dedications of new buildings. The business of running the city was in the hands of the city manager. Yet the image of mayor, as the presiding head of a city, was too lofty a post to have a Negro so dangerously close to filling that position. At least this seemed to be the thinking of Berry's political opposition, and in 1957 they were to use it to advantage.

This was a year of crucial race relations in the South between Negro and white, and a year particularly that was to erupt to violence in Little Rock, Arkansas, when an attempt was made to integrate the city's Central High School. It was an intense, angry demonstration, the backlash of which was felt 622 miles away in Cincinnati among the voting electorate. A vicious whispering campaign was already underway by Berry's opponents, spreading rumor that he had bought or was about to buy a home for himself and other Negroes in numerous Cincinnati suburbs and other predominantly white neighborhoods. It reached the finger-pointing stage on the eve of September 20, 1957, when a special election was held to decide whether or not to eliminate the city's Proportional Representative voting system. Opponents of the system resorted to open racial attacks, campaigning with such appeals as: ". . . you don't want a Negro as your mayor, do you?" The result was that when the election was over, the old system of Proportional Representation was voted out in favor of a new method known as "Nine–X," a plan by which the city elected its city councilman from the nine candidates receiving the highest plurality from among a field of eighteen. It was obvious that the chain of events was a well-calculated scheme to dispose of Berry as councilman and vice-mayor who would be seeking his fifth term in November. When the city voted for the first time under the new system on November 5, 1957, Berry, the lone Negro councilman, placed fourteenth among eighteen candidates in his bid for re-election. His only comment was: "I don't think the defection in my vote can be attributed to any particular group—except that the majority of white people did not want to return a Negro to office. " Two years later, in the election of 1959, Berry tried again to regain his councilmanic seat but as before the attempt was unsuccessful. His backers, including a "Citizens for Berry" group, sought to overcome the issues of racial prejudice in the election, blaming it specifically in a three-quarter page ad in the *Cincinnati Enquirer* edition of October 31, 1959. The ad stated: "Whether we like to admit it or not, there IS a color line in voting. That's what defeated Ted Berry in 1957—and might defeat him again. Fortunately, the great majority of this community's voters is both fair and intelligent. They vote for the man and his record, not his color. We are confident that Ted Berry's outstanding record after eight years in City Council has won him the firm support of more than enough voters to elect him to City Council; the great danger is that many of these voters may not vote—or will forget to cast one of their nine votes for Ted Berry . . ." The ad went on to make a plea for "10 extra votes per precinct for Ted Berry," but it availed little as Berry lost out for a second time. His opposition: racial prejudice—a cruel political foe. But as writer Leo Eagan once observed in the *New York Times*: "Politics is indeed a cruel occupation."

Chapter IV

DAWSON: THE MASTER POLITICIAN

IT matters not what standards of measurements are used, the man recognized as the nation's No. 1 Negro politician is Congressman William Levi Dawson of the First Congressional District of Illinois. Now seventy-eight and in the sunset of his lengthy and illustrious political career, Dawson is the venerable master of the game. He is "the old man" to his legion of followers; he is "the boss" to his immediate subordinates; and he is undisputedly a politician's politician. He has spent nearly forty years of his lifetime working at being just what he is—a politician. He has pursued it with a vigor that has demanded long hours, punishing schedules, and endless toil. His rewards have earned him local and national respect and a stout voice in the high councils of the Democratic party. He not only has held tightly to Chicago's Second Ward committeemanship for some twenty-four years, but is the acknowledged "boss" of six other wards as well. His power is further extended in his vice-chairmanship of the Cook County Democratic Central Committee and a similar post with the Democratic National Central Committee, both of which control patronage on their respective levels. In Congress he is chairman of the Government Operations Committee and supervises a budget of some one million dollars.

Yet for all his matchless success as a politician, Dawson scarcely fits the mold of the politician's image. He is reticent with newsmen. He shuns high-style living. He frowns upon bombastic oratory simply for the sake of being heard. He avoids publicity even when it may be favorable to him. And strangely enough, he prefers to be the listener in a conversation rather than the talker.

But his genius as a politician is evidenced in the well-oiled, vote-producing machine he has built up on Chicago's South Side, which is a tribute to his organizational ability. Some observers have said he is a politician first and a Negro second, and it may very well be that this sort of tact has helped perpetuate him in office. For as Dawson admits, "politics with me is a full-time business." "It is not," he says, "a hobby to be worked on in leisure hours, but it's a job—a full-time job that pays off only if a man is willing to apply the energy, start in from scratch and profit by his experiences." It is the only formula Dawson knows for big-city politics, and certainly it is one that he has learned well in almost half a century of making politics serve his purposes.

Like many Chicago Negroes, Dawson found the big northern city more attractive and promising than his hometown of Albany, Georgia. He was born there on April 26, 1886, the son of Levi and Rebecca Kendrick Dawson, the father supporting his family on profits from the barbershop he owned. It was sufficient to help young Dawson through Albany Normal School, but he chose to take various jobs as porters and waiters to help finance his education at Fisk University where he was graduated in 1909 with a bachelor's degree and the high scholastic standing in his class of magna cum laude. He was twenty-three at the time, and had never cast a vote. Chicago beckoned as a city that offered unusual opportunity to Negroes with professional training. In 1912 Dawson left Georgia for Chicago. In Chicago, Dawson studied at the Kent College of Law and Northwestern University, this time earning the money for his education by working as a dining car waiter on the railroads. He was admitted to the Illinois Bar in 1920 and began his legal practice as a mature adult of thirty-four years of age.

Dawson's entry into Chicago politics seemed to follow naturally his training as an attorney, but it was not until 1928 that he first sought a major elective office and this against Representative Martin B. Madden whom he opposed for his First Congressional District seat. He felt that this congressional post which Madden had held since 1904 rightfully belonged to a Negro inasmuch as Negroes comprised the majority in the wards that made up the district. "By birth, training and experience I am better fitted to represent the district at Washington than any of the candidates now in the field." Dawson was quoted as saying in the *Chicago Daily News* of March 2, 1928. "Mr. Madden, the present congressman, does not even live in the district. He is a white man. Therefore, for those two reasons, if no others, he can hardly voice the hopes, ideals and sentiment of the majority of the district." Dawson was only able to muster twenty-nine per cent of the vote in that Republican primary, but the showing was impressive enough to indicate that he could be a formidable foe in political matters. Of his early experiences he is quick to explain that he found few educated Negroes in Chicago politics when he first became active. "But I was willing," he says, "to give them [Negroes] the benefit of my education to help them do a better job politically." He admits that he was inspired by Oscar DePriest, from whom he learned the political ropes, eventually becoming one of DePriest's loyal lieutenants. "I recall," says

Dawson, "what great admiration I had for Oscar DePriest as a man who really had 'guts.' I remember seeing him put on a policeman's cap and uniform and drive a patrol wagon into the stockyards to bring out the Negroes who were trapped inside during the riot of 1919. He was respected as a former alderman, and he did what not a single policeman had the courage to do. Again and again he went into the stockyards, bringing Negroes out with him in the patrol wagon until finally he had rescued all of them from the white mob. His courageous action, undertaken at great personal risk, moved me to do something which taught me a lesson and something I rarely have done since. I sat down and wrote Oscar a letter. I told him I thought he had performed a great heroic deed and that I personally wanted to congratulate him. I also told him that he could always depend upon me for support in anything he would undertake in the future and that I was ready to stand beside him. Years later that letter turned up to my embarrassment. Oscar and I were then on the opposite sides of the fence politically, but he remembered that letter and dug it up and used it against me, referring to it in his speeches and waving it before his audiences wherever he went."

From a Negro viewpoint, Dawson approaches politics with the basic theory that where Negroes are sufficiently strong in numbers to hold a majority they ought to be represented in government by a Negro. He is distressed, however, by the fact that too few qualified Negroes aspire today to political office and that the great majority of Negroes must still be educated to politics. "We have the numbers," Dawson is quick to point out in discussing the Negro's role in politics. "We are the largest ethnic minority in America today, but we must be made to understand the power of the vote. The unfortunate thing about it is that the Negro, who was forced to come up under a system of slavery, was successfully brainwashed politically. The plantation masters allowed them to build churches and conduct services as long as the Bible was the only subject of discussion. Politics was taboo. The Negro had no place to learn politics. It was not taught in the schools. It could not be discussed in the churches. Yet Christianity itself would be the white man's greatest gift to the Negro. It gave him an abiding faith that somehow through his religion he would someday be delivered from bondage. And this faith, unshaken through all the years, is now finding its day of redemption. But we still must educate the Negro to politics. He must be made to understand that the vote is the best weapon the Negro has."

This innate political philosophy has characterized Dawson's lengthy career, but it has not led him into any blind avenues of ill-advised racial tub-thumping. Rather, patience has been the hallmark of his political endeavors, and positive action, executed in quiet, behind-the-scenes maneuvering, the pattern for achieving his goals. "I am a student of politics," Dawson related in an interview with the *Afro-American* newspaper in 1956. "It is a science of which no one should be ignorant. People should learn all about politics and how their government works. They should enjoy the right to vote and exercise that right. Everything we need as a people is between the four corners of the Constitution. Between those four corners of the Constitution we can work everything out. My years of experience have told me and I know. America is the greatest country on the face of this earth. I have always been grateful that I am an American. We are a part of everything here and all we have to do is let our buckets down where we are. We must make our way to the polls. We will crack Mississippi. We will be back in there putting them on the books by the thousands. Our right of ballot has been paid for in blood."

Dawson's great respect for the power of the vote and its worth to Negroes has been best summed up in his often quoted coined advice of, "Don't get mad, get smart," in answering Negroes who feel that the struggle for civil rights is a futile and hopeless one. In keeping with his thinking, he undertook to head up an ambitious voter registration project among Negroes in the South in 1953 and was successful in getting southern whites to see the wisdom of permitting Negroes to register. His plan was a three-pronged effort, first to get as many Negroes as possible registered in the South, second to get them integrated in the regular Democratic organization in his area, and third to get the white and Negro leaders in the southern Democratic organizations working together on candidates and programs for the best interests of both groups. To accomplish his purpose, Dawson himself went into the South, including his home state of Georgia, to make personal appeals to those white politicians in particular who had the power to give the green light to increased Negro registration. In Georgia, for example, he called directly upon political stalwart Herman Talmadge and pointed out that Negroes in Georgia were not arrayed against him as would be those who belonged to the Republican party. "They" [Negroes], Dawson argued, "are your neighbors. They work for you, they've helped care for your children. Just think what a bigger Democratic majority we could have if we could get these Negroes registered and voting in the Democratic ranks." To this kind of appeal, Talmadge, of course, nodded in agreement, and Dawson had accomplished his purpose. The theme of his approach was repeated in city after city in the South, and on one occasion in Memphis, Tennessee, in 1956 he told a Negro audience: "Quit crying about what some people are doing to you and go out and vote." He reminded the gathering that both political parties needed the Negro vote, and went on to say, "You're getting powerful, you have something they both need. If you have the vote they will make a beaten path to your door." A prime result of Dawson's efforts was that he was successful in getting the grass roots leaders of Negro and white Democratic groups in southern communities to sit down together, discuss their common problems, and conclude with agreeable working relations. Today, with civil rights organizations intensifying the campaign, and the Justice Department taking legal action in instances where voting discrimination has been shown, there are now more than one and a half million Negroes on the poll books of southern states.

To those who understand the basic ingredients of professional politics, Dawson is the embodiment of the organizational politician. The same unswerving loyalty he once gave the Republican party in his early career, he now bestows upon the Democrats. He is just as severe and bitter a critic of everything Republican as he is a vigorous defender of everything Democratic. He can be counted upon as a faithful follower of his party's leadership, and will vote according to his party's caucuses, even to the dismay of his friends and other Negroes who may not fully understand all the reasons for the stand he takes. The only explanation he may offer is one that seems to encompass his political philosophy: "We must play the game according to the rules. I always play it that way and I play with my team. If you are on a baseball team you stick with your team or you may not be able to play much longer. I believe in cultivating amity and harmony among people. Getting mad and calling names only widens the gulf between men. Such a practice lowers ones standards, shows a person to be ill-mannered, vulgar, a poor sport, and an ignorant man. How to put ourselves second and our team first is something we must learn. I would like to see us become integrated from inside the team. God gave me the key to understand men and to know them. If you learn to handle men, the right ones—all men for that matter—you can get what you want."

The powerful machinery that enables Dawson to remain in a commanding political position is a result of the many years of planning and manipulation that span Dawson's entire career as a Democrat. Once he had acquired the committeemanship of the Second Ward, he managed, by creating a compilation of obligations and loyalties, to extend his powers to five other wards as well. In 1943 he maneuvered to have one of his followers installed as committeeman of the Third Ward, then duplicated the same feat in the Twentieth Ward in 1951; the Fourth Ward in 1955; the Sixth Ward in 1956; the Twenty-fourth in 1961; and the Twenty-first in 1963. In each case, with the exception of the Third and the Twenty-first, the ward committeeman is also the alderman in his ward and together they represent control of the largest bloc of voters to be found in the entire state of Illinois. Each is a respected and formidable lieutenant in command of Dawson's forces, skilled in delivering the vote from among some half-million Negroes of voting age. All were hand-picked by Dawson to head their wards, and he will tell you, "I'm the granddaddy of them all." Today these powerful seconds-in-command are former track star Ralph Metcalfe, who is alderman and committeeman in the Third Ward; Mortician Robert Miller in the Sixth; George Collins in the Twenty-fourth; Kenneth Campbell in the Twentieth; Attorney Claude Holman in the Fourth; Charles Chew in the Seventeenth; and Joseph J. Robichaux, Jr. in the Twenty-first. Almost to a man they follow Dawson's leadership, although in the case of Alderman Holman, some defiance of the Dawson leadership has been demonstrated on more than one occasion.

It is difficult to assess Dawson's far-reaching power or the bulldozerlike strength of his Chicago Democratic Negro organization. Some idea of both, however, can be gathered from the Chicago primary of 1955 when the city's Democratic mayor, Martin H. Kennelly, sought re-election to a third term after eight years in office. A powerful hand in that decision to dump him was Dawson's. When he finally sought the endorsement of the Democratic slate-making committee, of which Dawson was a member, he was turned down in favor of Richard J. Daley, Chicago's present mayor and also chairman of the Cook County Democratic Central Committee. Kennelly himself told of the dumping in a campaign speech of January 30, 1955. He referred to Dawson as "a political boss," and said the two held different concepts of government. "I am not a boss," he said. "I refuse to be subservient to bossism." He then went on to say that he had appeared before the slate-making committee in a brief, three-minute, fifty-six-second audience, and gave this account of the proceedings: "That was the day I told them that I had always put public service ahead of politics and that I intended to keep on doing so. When I had concluded my statement there was utter silence for a matter of seconds until I said, 'I presume, gentlemen, it's unanimous?' Congressman Dawson responded to my question. He said, 'It's unanimous.' And I knew what he meant. He didn't have to elaborate for me. The 'word' was out: 'Dawson won't stand for Kennelly.' Obviously Dawson was in control. Control is very important to a man in the Congressman's position."

Dawson has pointed out that the primary reason behind Chicago's Negroes rejecting Kennelly for mayor was that he had failed to put an end to racial tensions in the Trumbull Park Housing Project, and that he personally had had only one personal experience with the former mayor. "I went to the mayor," he explained, "to ask for the removal of a Negro patrolman out South who had abused and beaten some Negro women. Kennelly told me that he didn't want politics in the police department, and that was as far as I got with my complaint."

When the votes were counted after the general election in April, Daley was the victor with 708,222 votes against 581,555 for Robert E. Merriam. The Dawson-controlled Negro wards had given the new mayor more than fifty thousand of his 126,667 margin.

Dawson's effectiveness as an organizer, coupled with the strength of the Chicago Negro machine wards, has played a vital role in presidential elections on several occasions. Extremely noteworthy is that election of 1948 in which President Harry Truman found himself in a desperate race with Republican candidate Thomas E. Dewey and the Dixiecrats' standard bearer, J. Strom Thurmond, who hoped to upset matters by getting just enough electoral votes to throw the election into the House of Representatives. Dawson organized a national committee among Negroes for Truman's re-election and raised thousands of dollars in campaign funds from Negroes all over the country. As Thurmond had intended, he managed to grab off thirty-nine electoral votes in the southern states that normally would have gone to a regular Democratic candidate. It was then necessary for the winner to get a majority of the 531 votes then in the electoral college, or 266 votes. Truman emerged the winner by gaining 303 electoral votes to 189 for Dewey, but it was an election that pivoted around the key states of Illinois, which held twenty-eight electoral votes, and Ohio, which had twenty-five. If the total of fifty-three electoral votes from both states had not gone to Truman, he would have had only 250 electoral votes, sixteen less than the needed 266. On the other hand, if they had gone to Dewey he would have had only 242, still not enough to show a majority, and the presidential election would have been in the hands of the House of Representatives, and doubtless to the advantage of the South. Dawson was credited with delivering an overwhelming Negro vote for Truman in his Chicago wards, thus helping to boost the slim, but vital, majority of 33,612 by which Truman carried the state. Truman was appreciative, so much so that Dawson could reach him for an audience whenever he needed it, and was a welcome visitor to the White House whenever he chose to go.

In the crucial 1960 election of President John F. Kennedy, Dawson masterminded another plan to assist the Democratic presidential aspirant. This time it was an organizational appeal to fifty thousand Negro beauticians, each of whom was held responsible for four votes for Kennedy. It was calculated to give Kennedy a built-in support of at least 200,000 votes, and in the final analysis, did, as the election results showed, give Kennedy the marginal edge in his victory over Vice-President Richard Nixon.

What must be understood, at this point, if at all possible, is the magnitude of Dawson's position in the government of America. He is, as it has been stated, a strict, disciplined, party-line politician, and it is rare that the public is ever fully informed as to what he does in behalf of the country he serves, the Negroes he represents, or the power of his seat in Washington. At most, unless one is a constant reader of the *Congressional Record,* Dawson's name might or might not appear as supporter of a certain important bill affecting the nation's welfare, and by and large he remains in the background. Few realized that even in January of 1949 when he became chairman of the House Executive Expenditures Committee that it was the first time in contemporary history that a Negro was named to head a major Congressional Committee. It meant that Dawson had the supervisory head of a body of about twenty-five members, whose powers included the right to investigate every executive department and independent establishment of the government, to see how they spent public monies, and to determine the efficiency of their operations. The committee may require any top government official to appear at public hearings on the conduct of his office at any level and require him to produce all papers, documents and books as the committee deems necessary. It also had the right to investigate complaints of racial segregation and discrimination within federal establishments wherever such bias is contrary to the Constitution. Moreover, it has the power to enforce payment of monies due the United States, and periodically receives and examines reports of the U. S. Comptroller General who accounts for all governmental spending. A tribute to the esteem with which Dawson was held as new chairman of the committee is seen in the fact that John W. McCormack of Massachusetts, then House Majority leader and ranking member on the committee, chose, rather than take a committee assignment, to serve under Dawson on the Expenditures Committee. In more recent years, with the Committee re-named House Committee on Government Operations, Dawson, as chairman, also has had the responsibility of issuing an inventory of what is owned by the United States.

While Dawson's obligations as an elected lawmaker and committee chairman dictate that he serve the welfare of the entire populace, he still is mindful of the fact that he is a Negro, elected largely by Negroes, and must keep tending the fires of Negro interests. In 1956, when the nation was strapped in the first cross fires of school integration, Dawson used the weight of his office to block an attempt in Washington, D.C. which hoped to show that integration of Negroes and whites in public schools was not a workable situation. The move was undertaken by Representative James A. Davis of Georgia, who sought through a sub-committee investigation into racial integration in Washington, D.C. schools, to prove that this would lead to mongrelization. Dawson, whose committee had to approve the allocation of funds for such a hearing, did not at first attempt to stop the proceedings, but went to the law books and dug up an obscure ruling that no committee could meet during a Congressional recess without the expressed permission of the House. Armed with this fact, and knowing that Congress was in recess at the time, Dawson went to the Speaker of the House, then the late Sam Rayburn. "You're right, Bill," Rayburn told Dawson, then tried to prevail upon him to hold off with his legal thunderbolt "for a day or two." Dawson's reply was an emphatic "no." "I'm going to break it up now," he insisted, and with that he marched into the midst of the committee room and passed out printed copies of the ruling which told the group that they were meeting illegally. The end result was that the meeting was broken up, and all monies it would have received for expenses, printing, transcripts, salaries, et cetera, were immediately stopped. "And do you know something?" Dawson now laughs, "I don't think they've received any money to this day."

It is rare that Dawson is as harsh in dealing with political opposition, rather his approach is of the silk-stocking texture, soft, quiet and effective. His speeches have been infrequent in Congress, but when he does take the floor, the chamber usually fills up to full quorum call. One of the most memorable was one he delivered on April 12, 1961, when he attacked the Winstead Amendment which favored segregation in the Armed Forces and would have permitted inductees to choose whether or not they would serve in an integrated unit. He related briefly how he had been born in the South, told of his service and wounds in World War I, and of the lack of necessary medical care because he was in a segregated outfit. Then he waxed eloquently to the subject under discussion: "How long, how long, my confreres and gentlemen from the South will you divide us Americans on account of color? Give me the test that you would apply to make anyone a full-fledged American, and by the living God, if it means death itself, I will pay it. But give it to me. Why should this body go on record at a time when we are fighting a World War to brand a section of its citizenry as second class? I have sat in the well of the House and I have seen you gentlemen from the South, and rightly so, applaud members of other races—non-white races—who were darker than I am. I have seen you applaud them, yet you will take me, a citizen of the United States, of your own flesh and blood, and brand me with second-class citizenship.

"If there is one place in America where there would not be segregation, that place is in the armed services, among those who fight for this country. Oh, I know how some of you feel; but there is but one God and there is but one race—all made in the image of God. I did not make myself black any more than you made yourself white, and God did not curse me when He made me black any more than He cursed you when He made you white. I would give up this life of mine to preserve this country, and every American in it, white or black. Deny to me today, if you will, all that American citizenship stands for, I will still fight to preserve our nation knowing that some day—under the Constitution of the United States—all of these restrictions will be removed, and that we will move forward before the world as one people—American people—joined in a democracy which shall set the pattern for all the world.

"I say to you who claim to love America, in this hour of its stress, that the greatest argument the Soviet Union is using among the black peoples of this world—to turn them against you—is your treatment of me, and Americans like me. No, I do not believe this body means to go off on this tangent, and I believe you who came from the South, if you would look back a little bit, would never, never again take a step to handicap any one of God's children for what they are. I believe that the South is big enough for all of us to live together in peace and in happiness if we can have but understanding; but we cannot have understanding if you array one against the other because of color . . ."

When Dawson concluded, most of the members rose from their seats and applauded until he returned to his seat from the well of the chamber. The amendment against which he had made such an impassioned plea was promptly defeated by a vote of 178 against segregation and 126 favoring segregation, with some white southerners joining in to send it down to defeat.

Dawson indeed is a man of many images to those who would seek to know him. There are times when one gets the impression that despite his great political achievements, he is a lonely man who is dedicated to traveling a lonely road. Politics has consumed his entire life in a kind of personal sacrificial manner that has pushed his home and family life into an obscure background. He was married in December, 1922, to the former Nellie M. Brown, who is today a registered Christian Science Practitioner in Chicago. She maintains an office in the modest duplex which is home to the Congressman when he is in Chicago, but rarely does she appear publicly with him on occasions of a political nature. They have two children, William L. Dawson, Jr., whose Chicago address is the same as his parents, and Mrs. Barbara Ann Morris. Both are precinct workers in their Congressman father's district, but like their mother, remain pretty much in the background of their father's political aura. When the Congressman is in Chicago for weekend visits, which may occur as often as two to three times a month, he can be found at Second Ward headquarters where he spends long hours listening to the people of his district on any complaint or matter they wish to discuss. This with him is standing policy and one followed every day he is in the city. He even has been known to be in ward headquarters on Easter Sunday and other holidays. "I am here to serve the people," he will tell you, "and that door (his office) is open to anybody. I will listen to anyone who wants to talk with me, and if I believe a person is sincere in what he has to say, I will try to help him. You can learn a great deal from listening to people, and it puts you in a better position to know what they want."

The impression Dawson gives is that he is a man of modest means, conservative habits, and simple living. His bachelor apartment in Washington, D.C., is a third-floor walk-up four-room unit in a four-story flat building in the heart of a Negro neighborhood. It is neat, tastefully furnished, but not at all in the storied image of plush quarters usually identified with a successful politician. Dawson spends his time quietly there, reading poetry [Paul Laurence Dunbar is his favorite] or going over books and papers with his colleagues. He is also apt to don an apron and take over the cooking chores in his Pullman kitchen, turning out a full-scale dinner for friends he might invite in. He may smoke or may not smoke, depending upon his mood. "Sometimes," he will tell you, "if I'm offered a cigarette—particularly from a white southerner—I'll take it. Then I'll stand there and hold it to make him light it."

Of his religion, Dawson usually smiles when the subject is brought up then lapses into a brief explanation. "There are some," he says, "who say I am a Christian Scientist and this may very well be true. I suppose I do have some leanings toward them. But when I was a youngster back at Normal College in Albany, Georgia, I became a member of the Methodist faith. It was one of those schools that stressed religion, and every so often they would hold revival services and the students would have to come up to the mourner's bench. On one of those days, I found myself on the mourner's bench while some of my classmates were outdoors playing ball. I could see them through the window, and it was my most earnest desire to get outside and join them. All around me, people were getting up and shouting that they 'had felt something' then would join church. But the longer I sat there, I not only did not 'feel anything,' but my desire to get out and play ball grew stronger and stronger. Finally I jumped up and shouted: 'I got it!' and ran out of there so I could get to the ball playing.

"In later years I became a Baptist in Chicago. It was during the depression and I became impressed with the good work a minister was doing there in a church on Wentworth Avenue. He was using his church to feed people who were hungry and out of work and this made a great impression on me. So I joined his church. When the time came for me to be baptized, I had to take off my wooden leg—I have a wooden leg, you know—and walked on crutches to get to the pool. I did all right until I got to the steps leading down into the pool, but when I got to that point I decided I could go it alone. I threw the crutches away and leaped in and probably would have drowned if the minister hadn't caught me. I attended that church regularly and would have kept on going if the minister hadn't permitted a white politician to come into his pulpit one Sunday morning and make a speech during an election campaign. I didn't think that was right. I thought it was wrong for the church to be used as a place for a politician to make political speeches. So that sort of brought an end to my connections with that church. And if people today say I'm a Christian Scientist, then I guess that's what I am."

Because Chicago's Negro South Side has mainly been the neighborhood for the flourishing and lucrative policy racket, Dawson has been a frequent target in the press in efforts to link him with gambling. He is quick to tell you: "I never took a penny from anybody," then will explain his attitude toward bribes and payoffs. "If you take money you become obligated. It puts you in the position of owing a favor. I've done favors for many people, some of whom I learned later were connected with the underworld, but I never took money. So that always placed me in the position of being owed a favor. For a politician those favors add up to votes."

To put it succinctly, Dawson's attitude toward gambling in his South Side bailiwick is one of understanding tolerance. It is best stated in an article by John Madigan in *The Reporter* of August 9, 1956, entitled: *The Durable Mr. Dawson of Cook County, Illinois.* Madigan quotes Dawson as saying: "Betting is a human frailty, but it isn't evil in itself. There's bingo played in the churches, and not too much racket is made about it. Race tracks are operated for financial benefit from sums bet on the races. How can it be wrong to bet on a horse at the track, where even the state takes a cut, and wrong for some poor fellow to bet on the same nag at the corner newsstand? Such hypocrisy is an invitation to the mob and the syndicate to try and corrupt the police. It makes people lose respect for them. It is particularly bad for a Negro district. Negroes don't create money. They usually go outside their area to work for it and bring it back into their community. And a corrupt system, growing out of gambling, drains them dry. Of course, the laws against gambling should be obeyed. But enforcement of one and not of another isn't liberty, it's license. If anybody is to profit out of gambling in the Negro community it should be the Negro. It is purely an economic question. I want the money my people earn to stay in the community."

The pace that Dawson set for himself in applying his energies to the demands of his political pursuits would undoubtedly have taken its toll with a less hardy person, but he has held up remarkably well in spite of his seventy-eight years.

Dawson is not a man to anger quickly, but if there is anything that draws his ire readily, it is a reference to him as an "Uncle Tom." Repeatedly he has lashed back at those who are critical of his tactics and among his most outspoken defenses of his methods was that which was contained in an interview with writer Ralph Matthews and carried in the *Afro-American* newspaper on January 26, 1957. "How is it," Dawson is quoted as asking, "that after fighting all my life for the rights of my people I suddenly awake in the September of life to find myself being vilified and abused, and those who know me well and what I have stood for are accusing me of being *against* civil rights? Not *for* civil rights? Why we made more progress toward civil rights under the Democratic Administrations under which I served and in which I had a hand in shaping the policy than ever in the history of the nation. . . . I have tried to fight for civil rights where it is the most effective, within the caucuses of my own party. I have helped to get good jobs for qualified colored people and many of the big posts which we hold in government today were obtained through this technique. I have also tried without hope of reward to spur the enfranchisement of thousands of colored voters in the South. This is the only weapon that will eventually silence the demagogues of the South. As long as the politicians of the South have a monopoly and have to account only to the white voters, we will always have obstruction and there is nothing the colored people can do to stop it. I have tried to concentrate my efforts on that front and never hesitate to go at my own expense to help any drive to help southerners get more voters in that area.

"Name calling and playing the grandstands is not the way to get things done here on Capitol Hill. If you want to get any advantages for our people, colored representatives must learn to play on the team. For this I am branded as an Uncle Tom and a lot of other names.

"You know what? One of my fondest memories is of the time when I was just a little boy when my father took me to Boston. As a special treat he took me to hear a lecture by the great Booker T. Washington. A great controversy was raging around the country over the philosophy of the education of the race. Many believed that the only solution to our problem was through classical education while Washington believed in industrial education. That night in Boston when Booker T. came to make his speech his opponents sprinkled the carpet with red pepper so that the people coughed so much it broke up the meeting.

"Yes, they called Booker T. an Uncle Tom. They said he was a detriment to the race and a traitor. But today the bust of Booker T. Washington is displayed in the Hall of Fame. Congress has just approved an appropriation to help preserve his birthplace for posterity while the names of his detractors have long since been forgotten. That is because the nation just caught up with the true greatness of Booker T. Washington. If the race had heeded his teaching and learned to do more with their hands, they would be dominating the great industries of America today instead of begging for admittance to many trades from which we are now barred. Yes, there are many ways to fight for civil rights. I have mine and others have theirs."

As the undisputed political boss in his South Side Chicago bailiwick, Dawson presides over his domain like a stern-handed father who rewards or punishes his followers as the need might be. His Second Ward headquarters, located in what was once a publishing plant, but now transformed into a political meeting hall after a $50,000 remodeling job, fairly hums with activity on election night. Workers stream in with reports of their precincts, and Dawson himself usually greets them to make a personal appraisal of how well or how poorly they have done in delivering the vote. Refreshments such as beer and hot dogs are available in the huge meeting hall, where on previous evenings the fare might have been a fiery pep talk delivered by Dawson himself. His subject may vary but his speech almost always concludes with a phrase that has become a kind of trademark with him. He will tell them: "Walk together, children. And don't get weary. Walk together, children, for there's a great deal coming by and by." It seems to sum up part of Dawson's philosophy, his constant reference to team work, harmony and understanding. If they are the keys to Dawson's success, they have served him well, for no one can deny that he is Dawson—the master politician.

Chapter V

THE MAVERICK POLITICIAN

UNLIKE Chicago's Congressman Dawson, who believes in strict adherence to the dictates and policies of his political party, there are some who do not hesitate to go against the grain of party-line politics. The most outstanding example, of course, is New York's Adam Clayton Powell, who has created an image of himself as the chieftain at the helm in the Negro's fight for civil rights. He has had a strong parallel in Detroit's Congressman Charles C. Diggs, Jr., who does not possess the same flamboyance as Powell, but is equally as unpredictable when it comes to remaining steadfast to party doctrine. Diggs is a comparative newcomer to national politics when measured against the yardstick of Dawson and Powell, but he is no novice at the game of politics. He, like Powell, has a knack for making headlines, and is quick to speak out in the interest of civil rights. He has ruffled Democratic feathers in this regard on several occasions, but, unlike Powell, has not gone to the full extreme of bolting the party to give political aid to Republicans.

Diggs got into politics in 1950 to take the place of his father, Charles C. Diggs, Sr., a Michigan state senator, who had been denied his seat on a technicality.* The younger Diggs, only twenty-eight at the time, stepped in to protect his father's political gains and won for himself the senatorial post in a special election held in 1951.

He was re-elected in 1952 to a second two-year term, then turned his ambitions toward Congress in 1954. The boundaries of the Third Senatorial District he represented were almost identical to the Thirteenth Congressional District, which for fourteen years had sent Democrat George D. O'Brien to Washington as its representative. Diggs challenged O'Brien in the August 4, 1954, primary, won handily, to get the Democratic nomination, then took on three opponents in the November election to win his Congressional seat. He won by a two-to-one margin over such a formidable Republican foe as Landon Knight, son of newspaper publisher John S. Knight. His other opponents were Karl Kurtz, a prohibition candidate, and Peter Goonis who was sponsored by the Socialist Labor party. It was an overwhelming victory for Diggs, who polled 64,716 votes, more than two-thirds of all the votes cast, and this is an area comprised of 55 per cent white and including such other minorities as Greeks, Jews, Mexicans, Chinese, Lebanese, Maltese, Irish and Italians. For Detroit's Negroes it was such a signal accomplishment that four hundred of them accompanied Diggs to Washington on a special train to witness the swearing in ceremonies which had to be done twice by the late Sam Rayburn as the gallery could not accommodate all the visitors.

* The elder Diggs had been indicted by a grand jury and convicted of taking a $150 bribe, ran for re-election, November 1950, defeated his opponent by a seven to one majority, but was blocked from re-claiming his senatorial seat.

As a freshman congressman, Diggs, then thirty-two, set out with great zeal to make himself known and heard. He was appointed to the House Committee on Veteran Affairs, and in his maiden speech before the House, made within a month of his election, lashed out at the Veteran's Administration for alleged discrimination in granting home and business loans to Negro GI's. The next day he introduced eleven civil rights bills, companions to a similar number introduced earlier in the Senate by Senator Hubert H. Humphrey of Minnesota. They were described as "equal opportunity" bills and covered a wide range of measures, among them fair employment practice, anti-lynching, convict labor and anti-poll tax. In a Baltimore, Maryland, speech, Diggs said in relating his presence at the trial of the accused slayers of Emmett Till where he was "an observer":

". . . And my mission to Mississippi also bears out my belief that although I am a representative of the Thirteenth Congressional District of Michigan . . . I felt I was elected to serve all of the people of the United States, and you can rightfully expect me to investigate any matter involving civil rights, civil liberties of any one in the United States, whether they be black or white." Diggs then went on to say that his father was "the first black state senator to be re-elected in Michigan's history," that he had been re-elected five times and was author of the civil rights law in Michigan which outlaws discrimination in public places. He then added that his father was a native Mississippian, having been born and reared in the cotton patches of Issaquena County, Mississippi.

While Diggs' presence in Mississippi at the Till trial was not intended to have any influence on the outcome—which, in fact, it could not—there was the feeling that, by his very presence, justice would somehow he pointed in the right direction. The accused men, John Milam and Roy Bryant, were both cleared of murder charges, but the tense, drama-packed, trial had world-wide attention. This alone was well worth Diggs' being there as millions of words were carried across the wire services, in newspapers and magazine articles, and Diggs was prominently mentioned. It was, as far as the public was concerned, a sharp contrast to the role of silence and "hands off" that Dawson seemed to be playing in the matter, although he was from Chicago and the boy's mother, Mrs. Mamie Bradley, lived in his district. But to those who were better informed, it was again a matter of "the old pro" versus the young politician, who had yet to make his mark. Dawson, with his years of experience, preferred the behind-the-scenes method of operation, and Diggs, with less than a year of service in his new role of congressman, needed to be projected into the forefront of national Negro leadership. The Till trial was the vehicle to help carry his name across America.

In the tradition of his determined campaign to secure civil rights for minorities, Diggs quietly acknowledged his newly won mantle as "a fighter against injustice," and let it be known that he would not be a party "tool" where Negroes are concerned. In the presidential campaign of 1956, he made public his criticism of his party's views on civil rights as early as November of 1955, while in Los Angeles to address a NAACP rally. In substance he said that unless the Democratic party could produce a candidate who favored a "progressive, liberal program," they would not win the presidency in 1956 no matter who the Republican nominee would be. "It is disturbing to me," he said, "that both Mr. [Adlai] Stevenson and Mr. [Estes] Kefauver have stated that they favor a program of moderation. I construe that to mean they favor moderation in all things, including civil rights, where drastic legislation and action are needed at once. If this is to be their program, I'm afraid they will get only passive, and not enthusiastic support from large groups of voters."

By March of 1956, Diggs' dissatisfaction with his party's proffered program of "moderation" in civil rights measures, became so intense that he himself threatened to bolt the party if "the Democrats did not stop pussyfooting on civil rights views." He further declared that he was undecided as to whether he would support the Democratic nominee, President Dwight D. Eisenhower [a Republican] or no one. When the eve of the Democratic convention in Chicago approached, Diggs, although pledged as a delegate to the "favorite son" nomination of Michigan Governor G. Mennen Williams, announced on July 28, 1956, his "whole-hearted" support of New York Governor Averell Harriman for the presidential nomination. In a prepared statement, he explained: "I have long been saying publicly that to win in November we Democrats must have a strong civil rights plank and a candidate with a forthright and inflexible position on this issue. In my opinion, the distinguished governor of New York, Averell Harriman, is such a candidate." He added, that if "my great governor G. Mennen Williams releases the Michigan delegation from its pledge to vote for him as a favorite son, I shall support the nomination of Averell Harriman." The eventual outcome of the convention, of course, was that Adlai Stevenson was again the Democratic party's standard bearer, and again went down in defeat to President Eisenhower.

What had been clearly established on a lesser political level was that Diggs was a kind of renegade who would not be held in harness and that he was able and qualified to make decisions in his own behalf that would be beneficial to him politically.

While Diggs has demonstrated that he is quite adept at playing the role of the political maverick, he has yet to equal the gymnastics of New York's Congressman Adam Clayton Powell in this regard. In fact, it is doubtful that any other of today's politicians can match Powell's ability to grab headlines or successfully maneuver against the grain of his party as he has done. He is to Negroes a symbol of leadership, a forthright spokesman who does not hesitate to speak his mind on any matter involving Negroes. He is the voice of protest, whether effective or ineffective, but it is loud and it has an appeal to New York Negroes who have sent him to Congress for nine terms. He is not at all unaware that he is forever on a soapbox and has often said: "I'm always on that soapbox. I've always got my mouth open—sometimes my foot's in it, but it's always open. It serves a purpose; it digs at the white man's conscience."

Powell, in his mid-fifties, has a handsomeness that appeals to women. He has been described as possessing a charm of "the pipe and tweeds variety," and has a flair for the dramatic that would rival most Hollywood actors. He became pastor of New York's Abyssinian Baptist Church in 1937 upon the retirement of his father, Adam Clayton Powell, Sr., and inherited a congregation of more than ten thousand, largest in the city and reputed to be one of the largest Protestant congregations in the world. His entry into politics was with the same dramatic flourish that has typified his career. He made himself known and heard in Harlem during the depression years when Negroes launched a boycott of white store owners who balked at hiring Negroes. The rallying theme was "Don't Buy Where You Can't Work" and Powell joined the picket lines as a leader to force the white merchants to give in. Thus established in the public's eye, he turned his attention toward the city council in 1941 and got elected on the American Labor party and the reformist City Fusion Ticket. He took his seat as an Independent, proceeded to operate as a "lone wolf," and was loudly heard on issues involving discrimination. When the Congressional district boundary lines were redrawn in 1943, Harlem, which had been divided among three districts, was now the heart and center of the Sixteenth Congressional District. Powell, under the New York law which permits a candidate to seek the nomination of more than one party, sought and won the backing of the Democrats, Republicans and American Labor party for the Congressional seat. He was elected without opposition in 1944, and took his seat in Congress in January, 1945, as a Democrat.

Scarcely had he arrived in Washington when he found himself in political disfavor. In that same year of 1945 the Daughters of the American Revolution refused to permit Powell's wife, at the time, jazz pianist Hazel Scott, to play in Washington's Constitution Hall. President Harry S. Truman's wife, Bess, was critical of the DAR for this action, but later attended a tea given by the organization. Upon learning this, Powell remarked angrily:

"From now on, Mrs. Truman is the last lady of the land." He had uttered only a dozen words, but they caused him to be excluded from visiting the White House for as long as Truman was in office.

In contrast to Chicago's Congressman Dawson, who makes no outward show of wealth, Powell has been characterized by Lerone Bennett, Jr., as being "a politician with an avowed fondness for old wines, fast sports cars and the company of beautiful women . . . a gourmet and a perpetual tourist who grows restless away from the calming influence of jets and steamships."

This man who is an enigma to almost everyone, who has been called both headline-hunter and prophet, demagogue and seer, further confused the political pundits when in the midst of a fury aroused by a government attorney's announcement that his (Powell's) taxes were under scrutiny, Powell grabbed still further headlines by announcing that he, a Democrat, would in the 1956 presidential campaign, support President Dwight D. Eisenhower, Republican. His announcement came after a visit with the President, and, in typical Powell fashion, was made on the White House steps. He said his reasons for switching his support to the Republican President was that Eisenhower had done more for civil rights and the Democrats had not heeded his request for a strong civil rights plank.

In campaigning for Eisenhower, Powell declared he would still remain a Democrat and hoped to swing other Democratic votes to the Republican candidate. His task, however, was not an easy one. He was dubbed "a Republicrat" by his opponents, and on one occasion, in Gary, Indiana, on October 26, was picketed when he attempted to make an appearance. The next day, accompanied by eight state policemen, he called a news conference in Chicago to declare that he would continue campaigning for Eisenhower despite the pickets. He said: "Neither candidate has come out as strongly as I would like on the issue of civil rights. Comparing the two men, I must commit what could be political suicide and throw my support to President Eisenhower."

His defection from the party was not without repercussions. Soon after the election was over, with Eisenhower being re-elected, Brooklyn Congressman Emanuel Celler, leader of the New York Democratic delegation to the House, announced in New York that he would seek Powell's ouster from his committees. He said he had been designated by House Speaker Joseph Martin to lay groundwork for Powell's removal from his No. 2 position on the House Committee on Education and Labor and his No. 5 spot on the Committee on Insular Affairs. Powell admitted that he expected a fight to remain in the Democratic party, and that there would be "a good chance to kick me out of my committeeship. But I have one thing in my favor," he declared. "There is no precedent. No congressman in the history of his country has ever been officially read out of the party." He added that he was convinced that House Democratic leaders were seeking to censure him solely because he was a Negro "who cannot be handled."

The matter finally came to a head in January of 1957 when the Eighty-fifth Congress was organized. The Democratic caucus had two other cases to consider besides Powell—that of a Massachusetts representative who had been jailed on income tax charges, and a Mississippi congressman who supported T. Coleman Andrews for President. It was the opinion of House Speaker Sam Rayburn that either all should be punished or none should be punished. The caucus therefore decided not to withdraw recognition, which meant that seniority and committee assignments were left intact. However, two of Powell's appointees on the House payroll were discharged by the House Democrats patronage committee.

Powell's tax difficulties, coupled with his defection from the

Democratic party, in 1956, placed him in the most vulnerable position of his political career. It was again congressional election year in 1958 and Powell had to seek re-election to the congressional post he had held for fourteen years. Under ordinary circumstances, the election would have been a matter of routine, but Powell had further earned the disfavor of Carmine DeSapio and Tammany Hall. The opposition stemmed mostly from Powell's behavior as a political maverick who was contemptuous of Harlem's recognized leaders. He shrugged off any decision they made in his behalf and remarked on one occasion: "They're all slaves to the white folks who control them. I don't care who they run against me—man, woman or in-between." The announcement of the party's choice was made by DeSapio in a news conference in Tammany Hall on May 15, 1958, that the Harlem district leaders, in a vote of six-to-one, with one abstaining, decided not to give Powell the Democratic backing. His explanation was: "They could not in good conscience support Mr. Powell because he is not a Democrat."

While Tammany Hall had no candidate to replace Powell, the news that he had been dumped by the Democratic machine headquarters had its reaction quickly in Harlem. Within two days after the announcement was made, it became obvious that Harlem's Negroes did not take kindly to the action. At a NAACP rally in front of the Hotel Theresa at the famed intersection of 125th Street and Seventh Avenue, Hulan Jack, Manhattan borough president, was roundly booed for ten minutes when he rose to address the crowd of some three thousand. It was not until Powell himself silenced the gathering that Jack was able to speak. The next day, Powell issued a warning that Jack and DeSapio better "stay off the streets of Harlem or we'll make it mighty uncomfortable." The NAACP took issue with him for the statement, and in a public announcement made by Executive Secretary Roy Wilkins, claimed that they wished to disassociate that group from Powell and that they did not condone "the extreme racialism raised by Mr. Powell." Later Wilkins backtracked, said the statement was "misconstrued," that the NAACP had not denounced Powell, and praised him as a leader who "had fought courageously for civil rights."

Powell, meanwhile, got his campaign going early. He let it be known that he was going to open "a political school" to train one thousand volunteer workers "who had never rung doorbells," and got out letters to registered Democrats asking them not to sign nominating petitions which did bear his name. He made similar appeals for money for his campaign in the name of "People for Powell," and vowed that after election he would break off completely with party bosses. It was evident that he was going to wage an all-out "lone-wolf" campaign, built around the hub of his Abyssinian Baptist Church with its ten thousand membership. It was common talk around Harlem that every parishioner was a campaign worker before election time, and that the membership made up 10 per cent of the registered voters in the district. Powell himself liked to boast: "I speak to more than four thousand people every Sunday—that's more than a Tammany District leader sees in a year."

The big question facing Tammany Hall, of course, was the selection of a Negro who could run against Powell. Hulan Jack backed away from the challenge, noting that his job as borough president was the highest elected political office ever attained by a Negro in the United States. There were such other names mentioned as Assemblywoman Bessie Buchanan, Thurgood Marshall, the noted NAACP attorney, and the Reverend James H. Robinson, who once had been an opponent of Jack's for the borough presidency. A final choice was made in New York City Councilman Earl Brown, an associate editor of *Life Magazine*, who hardly seemed a fitting combatant to equal the political image of Powell. He was a Harvard graduate, but lacked the bombastic oratory of Powell. He was smaller in stature, and while he had successfully held his seat on the city council, had, at times, been strongly critical of Harlem leaders. His terms were that Hulan Jack—with whom he was admittedly hostile—would stay outside the campaign and that Tammany Hall would underwrite the political costs of the effort, estimated in the neighborhood of some fifty thousand dollars.

The contest was between Earl Brown and Adam Clayton Powell, and it was one in which the racial appeal had its effect among the voters. Powell quickly seized upon the racial tenor, and with the accompaniment of Negro newspapers, managed to get across the idea that he was being punished by "downtown [Tammany] bossism." The *New York Amsterdam News*, through its columnist James Booker, noted: "There is a feeling in the community that whenever a Negro in politics gets to a certain height he is a target for political bosses to try to bring him down or control him." Another writer, Alfred Duckett, then editor of the *New York Age*, stated flatly: "The dumping (of Powell) was dictated by the Dixiecrats because Powell is a heartbeat away from chairman of his committee." Powell himself added some fat to the fire. On one occasion he said: "Now he (DeSapio) felt that when I was being clobbered on all sides, it was an opportunity to hit me while I was down, but I'm not down as long as the people are up and my people are up. And Carmine DeSapio's gonna get the lesson—he's gonna get a lesson in this—he's gonna learn that the day of bossism is finished, not only for the Negro people of Harlem, but all over town. People are sick and tired of bosses and Carmine DeSapio is going to learn the lesson of his life in Harlem and we hope that it is going to sweep all over this town and that people everywhere will throw off the shackles of bossism and we might have a Democratic party that will be true to the best principles of days gone by."

Joining Powell in the desperation effort was one of New York's most astute politicians, J. [for John] Raymond Jones, a shrewd, behind-the-scenes operator. Jones, a native of St. Thomas in the Virgin Islands, is known as "The Fox" because of his cleverness in political matters. He had become Harlem's political leader in 1943, had held such posts as deputy United States Marshal, deputy city housing commissioner and was secretary to two judges. He held a $12,500-a-year job as judicial secretary.

When Powell's defiance of Tammany Hall began to loom as a showdown fight, Jones, who had been relatively inactive, decided that it would be an excellent opportunity to step into the political arena. Powell seemed a good risk to win the election, and whatever rewards would be forthcoming, seemed worth risking a gamble. Jones had done well in real estate, so his decision was to resign his judiciary job and take over as Powell's campaign manager. The first major step was to make certain that Powell was not eliminated on the technicality of a nominating petition. New York law required that 750 names appear on such a petition, and they would have to be valid signatures that could not be thrown out by the courts. With the volunteer workers from Powell's church, trained in petition documents, a force of some five hundred persons was available to secure the necessary names. Tammany emerged ahead when petitions were filed, with nearly eleven thousand names for Councilman Brown compared to a little less than nine thousand for Powell, but Powell's petitions were ruled valid and he was guaranteed his spot on the Democrat ballot.

From this point on, the Jones-Powell bandwagon gathered steam-rolling momentum. The focal point was to keep Powell in the forefront, speaking and appealing to the minds and emotions of Negroes. There were Sunday afternoon meetings in Protestant churches, and in the last stages, sound trucks parading the streets carrying his message to the people of Harlem. The theme was: "I am being purged [by Tammany Hall] obviously because I am a Negro and a Negro should stay on the plantation." In a television program of June 6, conducted by John Wingate, he pulled out all stops. He declared that his interest in religion came about when he was nine years of age when, with his fingers, he scrutinized the brand mark of an escaped slave on his grandfather's back. "I ran away from the plantation in 1956," Powell said, "and now Carmine's trying to brand me."

Earl Brown himself sought to use the advantage of the column he wrote for the *New York Amsterdam News* to take a few pot shots at Powell as well as Hulan Jack. In one instance he noted in his column that there are three kinds of Negro leaders—the "loudmouth" who does nothing but shout protests, the "Uncle Tom," and the true leader, who works diligently and quietly in the interest of his people. It was obvious that he was attempting to categorize Powell as the "loudmouth," Jack as the "Uncle Tom," and himself in the role of the true leader. He was always quick to picture Powell as a "do nothing" Congressman, claiming he had done little for Negroes. He also accused Powell of being unwilling to work, saying: "Powell spends so much time in Europe you would think he's a Roman Senator instead of a Harlem Congressman."

From the beginning, Brown had been a reluctant, if not half-hearted, candidate who felt that he was certain to lose. Unofficial polls in Harlem indicated that he was right as Powell seemed to have the edge three to one. His chances did not improve as the campaign moved into its late stages and there were even rumors that Tammany Hall and DeSapio were ready to throw in the towel on him. Powell, meanwhile, stepped up the pace in the last two weeks of the contest. He made ninety-eight street corner appearances in the final two weeks, an average of seven sound truck stops each night for the fourteen nights. With him, to help attract attention, was a singing trio, although they hardly seemed necessary as Powell himself puts on his best shows before sidewalk crowds.

On primary day, August 12, the lines were long at many polling places despite drizzling rain. It was the biggest vote turnout in Harlem history with 23,343 of the more than fifty thousand registered Democrats in the Sixteenth Congressional District going to the polls. The results gave Powell a runaway victory for the Democratic nomination, winning by a vote of

14,935 to 4,959 for Brown. The amazing thing was that he won in almost all the districts, defeating every Harlem District leader who had dared oppose him. In Hulan Jack's own Fourteenth Assembly District, he won by a vote of 1,492 to 858, carrying even Jack's own election district by a majority of eighty votes. Powell, of course, boasted that he even carried the building in which Jack lived, then chortled loudly: "We beat Uncle Tom Jack in his own apartment house." Later he said: "This is the end of Hulan Jack. We will drive the Uncle Toms from Harlem." Then in a reference to Tammany Hall and DeSapio, said, "I don't need them; they need me."

Having successfully defeated the downtown organization in a most convincing manner, his election in November was virtually assured. In the gubernatorial race the contest was between the Democratic incumbent Averell Harriman and Republican Nelson A. Rockefeller, both millionaires. Powell, holding both the Democratic and Republican nominations, was in the enviable position of being able to endorse either candidate and yet not have his supporters split their ticket. All Powell and Ray Jones had to do was to sit back and wait and let the two contestants come to them to bid for their support. The decision came on October 7, when Powell called a press conference at his church to announce that he was backing Harriman and the entire Democratic ticket. He said: "Bossism is dead. . . . There is no more prejudiced attitude toward elected officials from the North as compared with those from the South. We are now a party of complete equality. The desperate need of the hour is for a strong and unified civil rights team in our state. This we find in the Democratic party." The pledges that had been made to him, he said, were that Harriman and DeSapio had agreed to give Negroes more and better jobs in the city and state, and that they used their influence to protect Powell's rights in Congress. He then joined Harriman as an associate campaign manager and was promptly accused by the *New York Age* of "being back on DeSapio's plantation."

On the November 4 election day it developed that Powell had picked a loser in Harriman. He himself won easily, garnering a total of 56,383 votes, 43,100 of them being furnished on the Democratic side, and 13,283 under the Republicans. His opponent, Councilman Brown, who had won the nomination as a Liberal Party candidate in the primary, got only 5,705 votes, a shade more than he had received in the primary. Harriman, Powell's choice in the contest, was rejected by the voters in a surprise upset by Rockefeller. The election, of course, settled all doubts as to whether or not Powell could successfully buck the organization, but although he had managed to get re-elected, there were two issues still up in the air. There was the matter of his status in Congress, and, secondly, the question of what would be the relation now between the Powell-Jones team and Tammany Hall. What Powell wanted was his patronage rights restored in Congress, a committee subchairmanship, if possible, and finally, some assurance that he would eventually succeed to the chairmanship of the Committee on Education and Labor.

The election victory did one thing for Powell, however, and that was to cast him in a new role of self-appointed "Kingmaker." He hoped to take over Harlem's District leadership and thereby place himself in a position to name Tammany's leader in the election of 1959. His plan was to control four of the sixteen district votes, and with such balance of power, dictate who would be Tammany "boss." He formed a new group called the Independent Voters Association, and at the same time opened four new club houses in Harlem. He and Jones both announced that they would run for leader in their own districts, and Powell, to demonstrate his earnestness, began keeping the hours of a district leader on Monday evenings when he was available in the club houses for all those who wished to see him. He was not being practical for neither he nor Jones could afford to risk losing in any contest for their respective district leaderships. DeSapio, although losing face with the beating he took at the hands of Powell, still held something of an upper hand in that he controlled the patronage jobs and contracts. Even if Powell and Jones won in their districts, he could still cut them off from patronage and contracts for Harlem, but DeSapio realized that he could not afford another fight with the possibility of losing. Jones, he felt, could be dealt with in any kind of compromise that would give him the political rewards he sought. It was just a question of what to offer him and how much. The only opposition to a deal between DeSapio and Jones was Hulan Jack and his followers, and DeSapio reasoned that he was no longer under any obligation to Jack since he had embarrassed Tammany in defeat at the hands of Powell. One thing was clear: Jones had made a successful comeback on the Harlem political scene and he was going to have to be rewarded. The full extent of his rewards, however, came on March 29, 1962, when Mayor Robert F. Wagner named him his top aide, through whom he dealt with all the Democratic political organizations of the city. It was an unsalaried post, but supported financially, as the mayor pointed out, "by contributions of various sorts." The precedent-breaking move officially named Jones a political secretary, but it bestowed upon him power second only to the mayor himself, and it was Jones' reward for again defying the regular Democratic party organization to support Mayor Wagner's bid for a third term. At the time, one Democratic county leader reportedly admonished Jones: "Don't you know you can't beat the organization?" To which the handsome, graying Negro replied with studied coolness and a flick of his cigar ash: "No, I guess you can't—that is except with a *better* organization." Then "The Fox" set out to whip together a force of assorted amateurs and volunteers that was largely responsible for returning the mayor to office. He conducted city-wide registration and petition drives which were as effective and successful as they had been in the 1958 Powell campaign.

It is interesting to note here that J. Raymond Jones was born November 19, 1899, in St. Thomas in the Virgin Islands. He came to New York to take a job in a defense plant during World War I, rather than accept a university scholarship which had been offered him in Europe. His interest in politics, coupled with natural leadership ability, soon found him in the forefront, speaking up for his American Negro "cousin" and establishing political clubs to compete in the main stream for political power in Harlem. He has been described as a man who is ruthless and his self-assurance is more apt to be mistaken for arrogance. But there are also those who will tell you that he is the kind of politician, who, after spending a week-end at his summer home in New Jersey, would stop off at Tammany Hall on Monday mornings with bouquets of roses for the workers. In the image of the American politician, he is a family man with two children—married to the former Ruth Holloway, a civil service worker, who in 1961 was named Collector of Customs in the Virgin Islands. They enjoy such typical New York interests as theater-going, book-reading and challenging each other over the chess board.

Of his own appointment as Mayor Wagner's liaison man, Jones admits to being an insurgent against "bossism." He was quoted in the *New York Times* of March 30, 1962, as saying: "I fought for Powell and I fought for the mayor for the same reason . . . because powerful men were trying to dictate who should represent the people." In 1963 he was elected to the New York City Council, further increasing his political prominence.

As for Congressman Powell, whose breach with Tammany seemed irreparable, he set out to accomplish the goals he had imagined for himself—that of controlling Harlem's leadership. In 1959, he organized a group known as the United Democratic Leadership Team, whose aim was to get more patronage jobs for Negroes. Then, with remarkable maneuvering, persuaded Hulan Jack—his once bitter foe—to join forces with him on March 22, 1960. Jack did not hesitate to make the new alliance with Powell. The truce between the two was realized in Jack's Municipal Building office where Powell had been summoned, and after an hour's conference they jointly announced their agreement to reporters. Part of the new arrangement was that Municipal Court Justice Amos Bowman and Harrison S. Jackson, Powell's personal attorney, were backed up by "the team" for election to two Municipal Court vacancies in Harlem in the fall. It was a kind of concession on the part of Jack who had been favoring his own attorney, Carson DeWitt Baker, for one of the posts, but who would now represent clubs in Powell's organization as law chairman.

In making the announcement of the political hatchet burying, Powell said that the harsh words that had been exchanged between him and Jack in the heated primaries of 1958 and 1959 had been "wiped out of our thinking and our minds." He also read a statement to this effect: "March 22, 1960, will be remembered as one of the significant dates in the history of the Negro struggle for self-determination. This is the day we stood up and told our town and the world that we are at last united." The agreement, he pointed out, marked the beginning of a concerted drive for more Negro patronage which was cleared through himself and Jack. In this regard he noted that although Negroes comprise 20 per cent of the voters in Manhattan, they received less than 5 per cent of the appointments, judges included. "This is a condition we have dedicated ourselves to correcting," Powell said, adding: ". . . and the doors are wide open for anyone—white or black—to join our forces in the area between 110th and 180th Streets, from river to river."

It is a tribute to Powell that he has the political skills to gather even his enemies around him when necessary. Call him maverick, call him demagogue, call him what you will. But there is no denying that to the Negro he is a symbol of defiance against the denial of his full citizenship rights. Powell, more than most of the "approved" Negro leadership seems to understand the masses and to be able to communicate with them. If there were no discrimination, if there were unquestionable evidence of equal rights for all, there would be no Adam Clayton Powell "to keep things stirred up," like a sound truck blasting at the white man's conscience. And to this end Powell has no peer.

Chapter VI

DEVELOPING THE POLITICAL SKILLS

FOR politicians like Dawson and Powell the skillful manipulations necessary to assure their perpetuation in office seem to come with ease. They are "old pros" at effecting the right maneuver at the right time. But the skills of their profession are not easily obtained by the novice, who soon learns that time and years must be invested before techniques can be mastered. Where the political machine exists, such techniques are more readily grasped for they are born of the system of organization and patronage. The latter device has been in existence for over a hundred years, ever since the nation's seventh President, Andrew Jackson, inaugurated the "spoils system," which gave rise to the slogan: "To the victors go the spoils of the vanquished." Prior to his election, in the forty years between the inauguration of George Washington in 1789 and the inauguration of Jackson, only seventy-four government employes had been dismissed and these for good reason. During the first twelve months of Jackson's administration, he dismissed more than two thousand employes because they belonged to the opposition. The same techniques apply today, and Dawson once commented on it in this manner: "If you had a friend you could reward with a job, wouldn't you give it to him?"

The matter of patronage helps weld together the wards and precincts which make up Dawson's district. His own Second Ward, composed of sixty-six precincts, is an organization composed of about twenty workers to each precinct, including the captain. Those who hold political jobs with the city, county or state are required to pay "dues" to the organization, amounting to about 2 per cent of their salaries. Moreover, each precinct must be self-sustaining, that is, it must support itself financially through such activities as "quarter parties" held at ward headquarters.

Some idea of the thorough organization of Dawson's Second Ward is seen in the fact that regular classes in political organization are held weekly for party workers. The classes, held each Friday night, are conducted by the organization's secretary, Lawrence Woods, a student of political science, and are dubbed by some insiders "Dawson College of Political Knowledge." Precinct captains are required to attend to be schooled in the techniques of organizing their voters, serving their needs, and becoming known to the residents in the precincts assigned to them. Although the classes are not year-round, they do begin in the fall [around September] and continue through the last primary election [about April].

Woods points out that "past performance" is not sufficient to keep a worker in good standing. "He must deliver the vote in every election," he explains. Drills are also sometimes held, and an illustration of the efficiency of workers in Dawson's Second Ward is seen in the fact that on one occasion fifty of them gathered at one of Chicago's twenty-story Lake Meadows buildings and canvassed it completely in twenty-nine minutes. The building, considered a precinct by itself, contains an average of three hundred families, and the crew was required to bring back answers to questions they had been supplied with. Woods also notes that whenever campaign literature or other information is to be made available to voters in a building of the size previously mentioned, a precinct captain can cover the entire building within twenty-four hours.

So efficient is Dawson at organizing that it was he, as we noted earlier, that set about the task of lining up fifty thousand beauticians nationally in behalf of Kennedy in the 1960 presidential campaign. His assistant in this undertaking was Woods, who explained that the strategy was to get each beautician to line up at least four persons for Kennedy. When asked why beauticians were chosen, he pointed out that it was much easier to work with beauticians because: 1) women spend more time in the beauty parlor than men do in the barbershop; and 2) women tend to take the advice of their beauticians.

How workers go about the task of reaching the voters and lining them up with their party is still a door-to-door, basic method of operation, but it is significant to remember that as times change and modern devices alter civilization's habits, so also must political techniques undergo change. It once was commonplace to hold mass meetings in large meeting halls to give politicians an opportunity to be heard, but this has given way to radio and television appeals which reach far greater audiences. Where intimate home gatherings in yesteryear could provide listeners for the politician's message, he must now face the challenge of Urban Renewal and high-rise, twenty-story dwellings in the large urban cities where only the precinct worker can carry his message and promises to the voters therein. In a city like Chicago or New York with skyscraper dwellings this procedure can be not only tiring, but frustrating work.

Why the political worker subjects himself to such demanding labor is a question that can be answered only on an individual basis. Aside from the job he may hold, the financial rewards in any given election are not as great as the public may suspect. In Chicago's Fourth Ward, for example, which is presided over by alderman and committeeman Claude W. B. Holman, workers are given "prizes" after election based upon how well they deliver the vote. In one primary election, a total of some two thousand dollars was given away by Holman to workers who had met such requirements as delivering "the biggest Democratic vote," or having "the greatest turnout of voters by a specified hour." Some workers, having met the specifications of the contest, received as little as ten dollars, but there were others who got as much as four hundred dollars in "prize money" for over-shadowing their fellow workers in the various election categories. For those "who failed to deliver" in this primary election—and there were some fifteen of them—it meant the loss of precinct captaincy.

The popular image which pictures the politician as a perpetual hand shaker and baby kisser is still counted among vote-getting techniques, but there are some precinct captains who have gone a step further. To stay in touch with their voters and let them know that they have some interest in their welfare, they resort to such sentimentalities as sending cards on Mother's Day, birthdays, or at Christmastime. When the occasion warrants they might also send flowers. Among those who hold elective offices such as alderman, state senator, et cetera, kissing is not confined merely to babies. This is held as a standard greeting for the ladies, particularly if they are elderly or tend to be unattractive.

One outstanding example of those who successfully employed the various political techniques is the late Edward M. (Mike) Sneed, a Cook County (Chicago) Commissioner, who first got elected to the County Board in 1938. Sneed extended his contacts with the public to visiting regularly the sick in hospitals and the elderly who were confined to the old folks' home. His beginning in politics differed somewhat from many of his contemporaries in that he had become a Negro Democrat long before it was fashionable for Negroes to belong to the Democratic party. A white hotel owner, for whom he worked as a bellhop, told him in 1928: "Sneed, as long as you work for me you'll always be a bellhop. With your abilities you should be doing something else." With that he gave him one hundred dollars and said, "Now go out and see what you can do for yourself and family." Sneed took his advice, got himself an introduction to Thomas Nash, then Third Ward Committeeman, and soon was made a precinct captain of the Democratic party. Later he became the first Negro Democratic ward committeeman, and during the depression demonstrated how to build an organization by promoting dances and boxing shows to raise money for distribution among the unemployed. Sneed died in 1964, having served sixteen years on the County Board.

It is obvious that oratory with the ability to move and sway masses of people is a most desirable skill in the art of politics. Among Negroes, the orator usually is pushed to the front in helping provide leadership for his party. Today's Negro lawyers, trained in the skills of public speaking, are a natural source of raw material for the political profession just as is the Negro minister whose success must depend upon his speaking ability. In years past, however, this was not always the case. An example was Chicago's late Roscoe Conkling Simmons, a professional orator, politician and writer, who is best remembered for his flowery eloquence; and to this end he was utilized extensively. During the Republican Convention of 1932 at Chicago, he was given the honor of seconding the nomination of President Herbert Hoover. A picturesque figure in swallow tail coat and wing collar, his eloquence is remembered although his speech was only of five minutes duration. He borrowed a quote from the great Negro abolitionist Frederick Douglass that "The Republican party is the ship and all else is the sea," then lapsed into his own flight of oratory. The crowd at Chicago Stadium burst into applause as he told them: "History will dip her pen in the dews of truth, and beneath the story of Lincoln's patience will write the story of Hoover's endurance." Despite his pleadings and hoped-for continued backing in the Negro Republican tradition, Roosevelt swept the nation in the November elections and Simmons, stubbornly loyal to the Republican party, soon found himself in political extinction.

On the other hand, Oscar DePriest, who made no claims to being a great orator, had the unusual faculty for making people listen when he talked. His delivery was in muffled tones, so much so that one critic said of him that he talked as though his mouth were full of hot pancakes. His greatest asset was the fact that he stood out in the crowd, commanding attention by his very presence with his over-average height capped by snow white hair. He did, however, develop a technique for speaking to Negroes in the South without, at the same time, offending whites. Witness, for example, a speech he made in June of 1932, in Elizabeth City, North Carolina, under the sponsorship of the Welfare Civic League. Details of his address were carried in the *Independent*, a local daily, which also carried a picture of him on its front pages. The newspaper, in reporting the meeting, noted: "The presence of a dozen or more white men in the audience did not cramp his style, and in a speech consuming the better part of an hour he said nothing for which he need apologize to either his own or the white race. In many parts of the country DePriest could pass for white." In his speech, this is what DePriest had to say:

"I don't know how much Negro blood I have in my veins and I don't care. I want to say at the outset that I'm not ashamed of my race; I had rather be a somebody among Negroes than a nobody among whites.

"The race problem in America will be settled on southern soil. And it is not a thing that is going to be settled in two or three decades; it probably will take two or three centuries.

"Southerners who have the most to say against social equality are generally the people who should have the least to say about it, for they have not practiced what they preach: the South has had sunlight segregation and midnight cohabitation. Look at the Negro race today. We came to America black, and now, as a result of white men, black men and women are becoming scarcer every day.

"The Negro must learn to use the ballot box to get his rights. If I lived in Elizabeth City, I would organize my race block by block and put them on the registration books. I would register two thousand to two thousand five hundred voters in Elizabeth City, and I wouldn't commit them to either the Republican party or the Democratic party. Between a southern, Negro-hating Democrat and a lily-white Republican, I would, as a rule, choose the Democrat.

"I wouldn't attempt to elect members of my own race to office: I would throw the strength of my race to the best white man regardless of his party label. When the best white people are convinced that you are for them, and when you have won their confidence and respect by demonstrating your ability to think right and vote right, then you are in a position to command their cooperation.

"More harmful to the Negro race than a hostile white man is the shiftless Negro who sells his vote. The Negro who sells his vote is not entitled to any of the benefits of government. And let me admonish you to pay your poll tax. A man who doesn't help defray the cost of the government he lives under should have no voice in that government."

The speech seemed caustic enough where Negroes were concerned, and apparently was not too objectionable to whites. But, in the North, particularly in DePriest's home city of Chicago, he was criticized for double talk. The *Chicago Defender*, in its edition of July 2, 1932, made this editorial comment:

"Congressman Oscar DePriest as a leader and advisor appears to be somewhat in the same dilemma as the young man who called on his lady love only to find her in the arms of his hated rival; he became so confused he ran from the house, jumped on his horse and rode excitedly about in circles before he got his bearings and set off in the right direction. The Congressman, as the spokesman of his people, has a different view for every section of the country.

"If he happens to be in the South, he advises his people to vote the Democratic ticket. If perchance his operations bring him North, then the Congressman at once becomes a staunch supporter of the Republican party. The psychology of the Congressman's political and mental aberrations is somewhat difficult to interpret.

"It is assumed that when the Congressman speaks in the North that he represents the Republican party. It is not quite clear just whom he represents when he speaks in the South. He has been quoted in southern papers as saying that 'the southern Negroes should vote the Democratic ticket.' The Congressman, however, has failed to explain to his southern audiences just how they will be able to get hold of the ballot so that they can vote since possession seems to be an essential element in the voting.

"The first thing the southern brother wants to know is how to get his suffrage back, not what to do with it when he gets it. If Mr. DePriest can tell him that, he will have solved the problem."

The politically astute former Illinois State Representative William E. King once had to reverse himself when it appeared that his support of a certain bill was not in line with his party's wishes. The late A. N. Fields, *Chicago Defender* political writer, brought it to public attention in an article in the January 23, 1932, edition of the paper. Fields wrote:

"Representative William E. King, on the floor of the legislature Thursday of last week, is said to have not only made a brilliant speech, but for irony and sarcasm had no parallel in this session of the legislature, and it was against the enactment of the famous Kelly bill having to do with the restoring of Chicago and Cook County to a sane financial status. Mr. King is said to have charged those who were behind the bill with attempt to wrest from the hands of the people their privilege of electing the board of assessors and review and to put that power in the hands of a few of their own henchmen.

"Representative King, in stentorian tones and with his breast heaving with emotion, declared that his race was about to be robbed of its God-given right of suffrage and that it was because of those rights that he had left the land of his birth in Arkansas, and by the grace of God, as long as he had breath he would fight against the usurpation of the rights of the people by the moneyed and privileged class. This brilliant attack upon the part of the representative was made on the floor of the legislature Thursday, January 14, 1932.

"It so happens that on Saturday of the same week, January 16, a meeting was called in the office of an outstanding political advisor, and at this meeting our brilliant young leader was told that all he had said against the Kelly bill on Thursday was really unintentional upon his part, and that the following Wednesday, when the bill was called up for final passage, he [Mr. King] was to vote for it. It is understood that the new leader offered some mild objections, but was told, 'it was not his to ask the reason why, it was his to do and die.' So we find the records disclosing that Mr. King, who was so bitterly opposed to the plan in the legislature, and who glorified himself at his last Friday night's meeting in his bold stand for the people's rights—we find Mr. King voting for this bill without even the courage to explain why he turned right about face."

While newspapers, both Negro and white, help create something of an image of the elected politician once he gains office, many Negro politicians seek to project themselves into the public eye. An exception seems to be Congressman Robert N. C. Nix, representative from Pennsylvania's Fourth District, who was elected in 1958 in Philadelphia and became the fourth Negro elected to Congress in the contemporary period. Unlike Powell, who rarely misses an opportunity to be heard and gain for himself newspaper space, or Diggs, who attracted national attention during the Till trial, Nix has been unusually quiet. He was elected to fill the unexpired term of Earl Chudoff, who resigned to become a Common Pleas Court judge. Nix won easily in a special election held on May 20, 1958, polling 13,572 votes to 7,505 for his Republican opponent, Cecil B. Moore. It was also the same date of the primary, and Nix, seeking a full term before even taking office, gained the nomination in this Democratic race, defeating Harvey N. Schmidt by a vote of 16,341 to 8,466. His victory was his reward for twenty-five years of organizational work with the Democratic party. An attorney since 1925, he was, at the time of his election, a special deputy attorney general assigned to the escheats division of the state Department of Revenue. He had been a committeeman in Philadelphia's Forty-fourth Ward since 1932, and ward chairman of the Forty-fourth Ward executive committee since 1950.

Like Diggs, Nix was accompanied by a delegation of well-wishers, who traveled to Washington with him aboard the Nix Congressional Special for the swearing-in ceremonies on June 4, 1958. When the new Pennsylvania representative, then fifty-three, took his oath of office, the entire body, both Democrats and Republicans, rose and gave him a standing ovation of welcome at the end of the ceremony. Then, in an unusual demonstration, the South Carolina delegation, remembering that he was born in Orangeburg, South Carolina, came to him in a body to congratulate him.

It was nearly two years before Nix became involved in his first major civil rights fight on Capitol Hill. In February of 1960 he got into what was described as "a quarrel on paper" with Senator Olin Johnston of South Carolina over Negro voting rights in their home state. Nix had reprinted in the *Congressional Record* an article which charged that southern Negroes were not permitted to vote, and as a result, men like Johnston were elected. Johnston lashed back in a floor speech, took issue with the charges and claimed that more than a hundred and fifty thousand Negroes voted in his state and many of them voted for him.

It is rare that a politician can remain politically active over a period of time once his party has been voted out of power, but one of the few exceptions to this is Chicago's Reverend Archibald Carey, a brilliant speaker, who is respected not only for his oratory but his political prowess as well. Carey, a rock-ribbed Republican, is pastor of the oldest Negro church in Chicago, the Quinn Chapel African Methodist Episcopal, which celebrated its 116th anniversary on July 22, 1962. It was formerly pastored by his father, the late Bishop Archibald Carey, Sr., an early Chicago politician. Like the father, the younger Carey has enjoyed a distinguished political career, despite the fact that he has remained Republican in the face of Chicago's powerhouse Democratic machine. He first projected himself on the political scene in 1947 when he was elected to Chicago's city council, a post he held for eight years until 1955, when Dawson's Democratic organization hoisted track star Ralph Metcalfe into office to replace him. In 1953 he was appointed First Alternate Delegate to the Eighth General Assembly of the United Nations, representing the United States on the Legal Committee. National recognition came to him on January 18, 1955, when President Eisenhower, by Executive Order 10590, created the President's Committee on Government Employment Policy and named Carey vice-chairman. He succeeded to the chairmanship of the committee on August 5, 1957, replacing Chicago accountant Maxwell Abbell who resigned, and it marked the first time in history that a Negro had chaired a President's Committee. Serving with him were such outstanding personalities as Branch Rickey, who integrated baseball by hiring Jackie Robinson, Henry Cabot Lodge, Jr., and James Zellerbach of Crown-Zellerbach Paper Company.

Archibald Carey could be classified as a "peculiarity" in politics in that he commands the respect of fellow politicians whether they be Democrat or Republican. He has successfully mixed the business of politics with his ministerial duties at his church, as well as his law practice, and has managed to maintain one of the most "spotless" political reputations in the nation. Chicago daily newspapers consistently have been laudatory in appraisals of his governmental assignments, and he has had their blessings and backing on numerous occasions.

On March 19, 1955, the *Chicago Daily News* took notice of his last speech in the City Council with this commentary in its columns:

"Alderman Archibald J. Carey (3rd), the only ordained minister in the City Council, and the council's finest orator, turned his final aldermanic address into a friendly, kindly farewell sermon. . . . His appearance at Friday's session marked the last time he would sit for the city's Near South Side Ward." The paper then went on to quote excerpts from Carey's farewell message. "When I entered the council I was pastor for 1,600 members of my church," he was quoted as saying. "I soon found out that I had become pastor for 90,000 constituents. . . . I learned a great deal here—the City Council is one of the greatest schoolrooms I ever attended. . . . I have gained respect, without exception, for the way the aldermen serve their constituents and for their diligence." In a more candid observation, Carey noted that "in my eight years in the council I have observed that there is no place for inferior men or those of petty attitude. Too often aldermen forget they are elected for two purposes—not only to present the petitions and prayers of their ward, but also to represent the city at large. There are local aldermen and there are City Fathers. Too often we fail to measure up to our duties as City Fathers." He concluded with a proposal that a referendum be held the next year to grant aldermen a pay raise from five thousand dollars annually to eight thousand dollars. "I favor a twelve thousand dollar salary," he explained, "but the state statutes have placed a limit on the ceiling." His proposal, however, was not accepted.

Archibald Carey is steeped in political know-how and the articulation of speech, but he lacks the organizational strength behind him. His battle is like that of the fisherman with the leaking rowboat, who cannot devote his energies to fishing for bailing out the water from his inundated craft. He could be the Republican Dawson—if there should be such a counterpart—but he is the kind of man who insists upon playing politics on the highest level and with the greatest attention to the needs of the Negro community. Even in defeat, he has demonstrated his charm and humility, the essential assets of the successful politician. In a letter to the *Chicago Daily News*, following the loss of his aldermanic post, Carey publicly thanked his supporters and had kind words to say of his opponent. The letter, published on February 28, 1955, stated:

"A surprising number of people have been kind enough to express to me their disappointment that I was not re-elected to the City Council. On second thought, this should not surprise me because so many people were kind enough to help me in so many ways. Church people, labor groups and single individuals trudged the streets and rang doorbells to supplement the small Republican organization which was working for me. And the newspapers, without exception, were most generous in stressing my virtues while overlooking my faults. All of this help shows clearly when the vote is analyzed. The Third Ward went overwhelmingly Democratic, but while it voted Democratic five-to-one for mayor, it only voted two-to-one on the alderman. My friends get comfort, if small, from the fact that in the Third Ward, I, a Republican, received twice as many votes as other Republicans there.

"The new alderman, Ralph Metcalfe, has made a fine record as an athlete and now has an opportunity to make an even finer record in public office.

"I just want to thank so many who did so much to help me. I trust I shall always merit their confidence. . . ."

Carey's ability as an orator has earned for him the distinction of being the third most-requested Republican speaker in the nation. His party became keenly aware of his skills in this regard in 1952 during the Republican National Convention at

Chicago when he electrified the gathering with his brilliant oratory. One newsman, Price Day of the *Baltimore Sun*, was so impressed he chose to pay warm compliments to the Chicago minister-politician in his convention story of July 8. Day wrote: ". . . Their [the delegates] psyches had been shocked to the depths when their keynote speaker, billed in advance as the greatest thing since William Jennings Bryan in 1896, gave an address from which today they could not recall one quotable phrase.

"They wanted a moment of peace, quiet and background music.

"Those who sought rest in the convention hall, however, were nudged into wakefulness at the close of the short daytime session by a man whose name most of them had never heard.

"When Archibald Carey, Jr., a Chicago city councilman, went to the rostrum, the two-thirds of the delegates who had ventured through the rain out to the hall were listening with no more attention than they had given to the earlier speakers, Senator Styles Bridges of New Hampshire, Representative Marguerite S. Church of Illinois, and Senator James P. Kem of Missouri.

"But when Carey, . . . told them that the Negro vote of the country was 'the most flexible and sensible of the American electorate,' a few of them began to listen.

"Then more listened, and the speaker had the attention of the whole hall as he went into his peroration.

" 'From every mountainside,' the Reverend Mr. Carey pleaded as his waving left arm knocked a glass of water into the lap of a reporter for the *Associated Press*, 'let freedom ring.'

" 'Not only from the Green Mountains and the White Mountains of Vermont and New Hampshire, not only from the Catskills of New York, but from the Ozarks in Arkansas, from Stone Mountain in Georgia, from the Great Smokies of Tennessee and from the Blue Ridge Mountains of Virginia—

not only for the minorities of the United States, but for the persecuted of Europe, for the rejected of Asia, for the disfranchised of South Africa and/or the disinherited of all the earth, may the Republican party, under God, from every mountainside, let freedom ring.'

"By that time, the delegates were standing, and when the Reverend Mr. Carey finished, they cheered him. It was the convention's first spontaneous demonstration. . . ."

During the Eisenhower administration, Carey was a frequent visitor to the White House, a privilege he had earned in the 1952 presidential campaign when he traveled more than twenty-one thousand miles across the nation on a speaking tour in Eisenhower's behalf. Among his most cherished possessions are several letters from the former President, commending him for his political service.

There are—and have been—a hard core of Negro politicians, who, like Carey, refuse to switch their allegiance from Republican to Democrat and have been remarkably successful at getting elected to political office. One outstanding example is the late Charles W. Anderson, Jr., of Louisville, Kentucky, whose career, before his death in June of 1960, spanned twenty-five years of working in behalf of the Republicans. He first was elected to Kentucky's legislature in 1935 while still a young man of twenty-five and gained the distinction of being the first Negro ever elected as a member of that body. He was re-elected for six consecutive terms, or a total of twelve years, and finally in 1945, returned to office without either Democratic or Republican opposition. In May, 1946, he resigned his post in the state legislature to establish another first, this time accepting the position of Assistant Commonwealth's Attorney for the Thirtieth Judicial District of Kentucky. Again it marked the first time that a Negro attorney was elevated to such a position in Kentucky or the South. At the time of his death, Attorney Anderson was a member of the United States delegation to the United Nations. He was killed instantly in a Bagdad, Kentucky railroad crossing collision, bringing an abrupt end to the fifty-three-year-old attorney's colorful and varied political career.

Negro politicians have fared well in Kentucky, particularly in Louisville where a Negro has sat on the city council since 1945. In that year, the late Eugene S. Clayton was the first Negro to gain election to a city aldermanic post on the Republican ticket, and it marked the first time since Reconstruction that a Negro in the South had won a seat on the city council. His term extended for a two-year period, and the post was later filled by the late W. W. Beckett, a Negro mortician who was a successful Democratic candidate.

It is a basic truth that of all the skills a politician must develop, he first of all must be able to attract votes. There have been exceptions when Negroes have been elevated to lofty positions where such appointments attract votes for the party rather than for the politician. This was true in the case of the late J. Ernest Wilkins, a Chicago attorney, who, in March of 1954, was named by President Eisenhower to the sub-cabinet post of Assistant Secretary of Labor. Wilkins, who was sixty at the time, and a lifelong Republican, could hardly be considered in the image of the tub-thumping, office-seeking politician and it came as a mild surprise to some when Eisenhower named him to the high governmental post. Without a doubt the appointment helped attract some Negroes to the Republican fold, but more than that it added prestige to the image of the party as a whole. He was an intellectual, a Phi Beta Kappa, and had served as vice-chairman of President Eisenhower's Committee on Government Contracts in 1953 and as president in 1955 of the President's Committee on Government Employment Policy. The Senate Labor Committee applauded the appointment with such comments as this from its chairman, Senator H. Alexander Smith of New Jersey: "We're interested in his qualifications, not the color of his skin . . . I am entirely in favor of the selection of a Negro where he qualifies. The principle is definitely sound."

While Wilkins served with zeal in his new twenty-thousand-dollar-a-year post, his career came to an abrupt end four years later in November of 1958 when he handed in his resignation. It was reported at the time that he had been asked to resign by President Eisenhower so that the job could be given to George C. Lodge, son of chief United Nations delegate Henry Cabot Lodge, Jr. This charge was later denied by Secretary of Labor James P. Mitchell, but Lodge did succeed to Wilkins' post after his resignation. Two months later, Wilkins died of a heart attack in Washington, D.C.

Occasionally a politician is able to give his career a mighty thrust if a combination of circumstances arise in his favor. In this regard, Chicago attorney William Sylvester White, Jr., is a particular standout in that he was able to project himself into an Illinois cabinet post during the gubernatorial election of 1960. His father, William Sylvester White, Sr., was one of the early Negro Democratic leaders, having served as supervisor of Sixth Ward precinct captains in the mayoral campaign of Anton J. Cermak. The younger White had labored in Chicago's Fourth Ward as a precinct captain, and as a result was rewarded with various governmental jobs, the first of which was an appointment in 1939 as Assistant United States Attorney for the Northern District of Illinois. From 1955 to 1956 he served as Assistant State's Attorney, and in 1957 was named attorney for the City Department of Investigation, a post from which he was later elevated to Deputy Commissioner. In 1960, when former Judge Otto Kerner successfully hurdled the Democratic primaries to secure the nomination for governor, White, who had known him from his days in the United States Attorney's office, began a campaign in his behalf. He helped organize a South Side group to support Kerner, raised funds to finance his own organization, and saw his candidate sweep into office in November. His efforts were rewarded with the fifteen-thousand-dollar-a-year position of State Director of Registration and Education, a post of cabinet rank, which has the responsibility for granting licenses to a variety of public agencies and individuals, including physicians and real estate brokers. He thus becomes the only Negro in the United States to enjoy a governmental position on a governor's cabinet level, yet not hold a higher political job than that of precinct cabinet. But such are the rewards of exercising political skills, and it is to such an end that the politician devotes his energies.

Chapter VII

THE WOMAN IN POLITICS

TO the general public it appears that politics belong to the male in that almost always the candidate for office is a male and the political titles of office have been given masculine designations. It probably comes as a surprise to many that the majority of political workers are women, and that among Negroes they outnumber men in performing the grass roots tasks necessary to political success. Congressman Dawson has said that "the Negro woman has been the salvation of Negroes politically." In his opinion, "they [women] are unbending, cannot be easily swayed, and cannot be bought. This is in contrast to the Negro male who is susceptible to money." In Dawson's own Second Ward organization in Chicago women workers outnumber men by about four to one.

The rise of the woman politicially goes back nearly one hundred years to 1869 when Wyoming, then a sparsely settled territory, established women's suffrage although there were few women in the area at the time. Colorado followed suit twenty-four years later in 1893, then Utah and Idaho in 1896, Washington in 1910, and finally the remainder of the states west of Colorado granted full suffrage to women. The Negro woman has been the mainstay of the Negro man in politics almost since the post-Civil War South. Among the first was Ida B. Wells, who was born in Holly Springs, Mississippi, in 1868. She was militant and loudly vocal in behalf of Negroes, an attribute which probably stems from the fact that she was born of slave parents. When she was fourteen her parents died, leaving her with the responsibility of rearing five younger brothers and sisters. She had been attending one of the schools operated at the time by the Freeman's Aid Society of the African Methodist Episcopal Church and decided that she would get a job teaching school. She taught in a country school for a few years then moved to Memphis, Tennessee, where she sought more education and a teaching position in the city schools.

Of her career as an early Negro woman politician, Harold F. Gosnell has this to say in his book, *Negro Politicians:* "One of the most militant of these was the late Mrs. Ida Wells Barnett, a woman of powerful frame, whose eyes gleamed with an inner fire . . . (When) she became a contributor to one of the local newspapers (in Memphis) . . . one of her articles concerning the teacher's moral qualifications caused her dismissal from the school system. This forced her into journalistic work, where she soon acquired a reputation for fearless writing. When two of her friends who ran a store just outside the city limits were lynched because they defended themselves against what they regarded a hostile attack, she fled to Oklahoma and continued her editorial work by mail.

"One of her editorials brought such a storm of protest among the whites in Memphis that a mob destroyed her printing plant and threatened death to anyone who attempted to publish the paper again. Mrs. Barnett began a career as a lecturer on lynching, traveling extensively in both England and the United States. Typical of her vigor of expression is the following passage on the value of the franchise.

"With no sacredness of the ballot there can be no sacredness of human life itself. For if the strong can take the weak man's ballot, when it suits his purpose to do so, he will take his life also. . . . The Mob says: 'This people has no vote with which to punish us or the consenting officers of the law, therefore, we indulge our brutal instincts, give free rein to race prejudice and lynch, hang, burn them when we please.' "

Gosnell goes on to say of her: "Coming to Chicago at the time of the World's Fair in 1893, Mrs. Barnett became active in movements for racial justice. She achieved a wide reputation as a social worker, an agitator for woman suffrage, a promoter of colored women's clubs, and a Republican party organizer. In 1909 she took an active part in urging Governor Charles S. Deneen to take vigorous action against the sheriff of Alexander County in whose jurisdiction a Negro had been lynched. . . . Mrs. Barnett's burning zeal for Negro rights and her untiring energy devoted to the cause of greater political power for her people were the products in part of her experiences in the South."

Ida B. Wells possessed the kind of die-hard fighting spirit that has had its carry-over even among today's women politicians. There is little doubt that much of this vigor brimmed over to engulf her husband, Ferdinand Barnett, who was to distinguish himself as founder and publisher of Chicago's first Negro newspaper, *The Conservator*. He was an 1880 graduate of the Chicago College of Law, and earned for himself several political "firsts," among them: first Negro appointed Assistant State's Attorney in 1898 and first Negro to seek a Municipal Court Judgeship (in 1906) although he lost by three hundred votes in a contested recount.

The strides which Negro women politicians have made in placing themselves in elective offices have not kept pace with their male counterpart. There are only a score or so of Negro women who have made a dramatic success at politics, although they work diligently to aid the party of their choice. Even today there are less than a dozen across the nation who have gained elective office in the sense that they are political constituents. Mostly they have elevated themselves to positions of power within their parties where their influence is felt.

By an *Ebony Magazine* survey (July, 1962), out of sixty-eight Negro judges, there are only three women. These three were appointed to their judicial posts. They are: Domestic Relations Court Judge Jane M. Colin of New York City, who was first appointed in 1939 by Mayor F. H. LaGuardia. Her term extends for thirty years until 1969. Mrs. Juanita Kidd Stout of Philadelphia's County Court is perhaps the highest paid Negro woman in the judiciary. Her salary is $22,500 per year and her term of office extends until 1970. Vaino Spencer is judge of the Los Angeles Municipal Court, commanding a salary of $18,950 and hearing, primarily, traffic cases. The Democratic party in Los Angeles can take a considerable amount of credit for Judge Spencer's appointment which came in 1961 after many years of intense effort.

Following the survey of July, 1962, referred to above, Attorneys Marjorie Lawson of Washinton, D.C., and Edith Sampson of Chicago joined the ranks of lady jurists. Attorney Lawson was appointed judge in the Juvenile Court of the District of Columbia at an annual salary of $17,500. Edith Sampson, former alternate delegate to the United Nations, and an attorney on the staff of the Corporation Counsel of the City of Chicago, is the first to achieve the elusive honor of being placed on the slate to run for a judgeship and be elected. Mrs. Sampson was elected in the regular November, 1962, judicial race to fill a two-year vacancy on the Chicago Municipal Court bench at an annual salary of $19,500.

Attorney Edith Sampson is the kind of Negro woman who can be used most effectively in politics when it comes to boosting the American image. She has a deep throaty voice, which she uses with considerable vigor when addressing audiences or participating in debate. She is able to boast that she earned her law degree from Chicago's John Marshall Law School by attending night classes and working in the daytime as a probation officer for the Juvenile Court of Cook County. Later, she became the only woman ever to receive a master's degree in law from the graduate school of Loyola University. Against these accomplishments, she could contrast her early childhood in Pittsburgh, Pennsylvania, where she was born one of eight children to parents who had no more than grade school education. She could mention that her father managed a cleaning and dyeing establishment and that her mother operated a part-time millinery and false hair business. It was in this business that Attorney Sampson helped out as a child, wiring the hat frames and twisting switches of hair. At fourteen, she held her first job—in a fish market, scaling and boning fish after school.

In 1950, when President Harry Truman named her as a member of the United States delegation to the United Nations it was a move to help disprove Russian propaganda claims that Negroes are denied high office in the United States. Attorney Sampson already had made her qualifications evident the year before in 1949 as a member of the World Town Hall Seminar. It was a group organized by George V. Denny, Jr., moderator of the Town Meeting of the Air, which was composed of representatives of twenty-eight national organizations. Their mission was a seventy-two-day journey abroad, during which Mrs. Sampson, representing the National Council of Negro Women, visited twenty countries, including fourteen world capitals, participating in open debate on political questions. Once in India, during the tour, she was asked directly whether Negroes have equal rights in America. Her reply was: "My answer is no, we do not have equal rights in all parts of the United States. But let's remember that eighty-five years ago Negroes in America were slaves and were one hundred per cent illiterate. And the Negro has advanced further in this period than any similar group in the entire world. . . .

"Does this mean that I am satisfied? No, not by a long shot! We will never be satisfied until racial barriers are lifted, and we have full and complete integration. But we know that, under a democracy, we have freedom and opportunity to better existing conditions."

Such diplomacy not only made her ideally suited for her role in the United Nations, but in January of 1962 she was called upon again to represent the United States in discussions abroad. This time she was chosen on the twenty-member U. S. Commission to participate in the two-week Atlantic Convention of NATO nations, which was held in Paris, France beginning January 8. The convention was a gathering of ninety-eight outstanding citizens appointed by legislatures of the fifteen nations represented in the North Atlantic Treaty Organization. Its business was to provide an opportunity for non-governmental leaders to seek ways of advancing democratic freedom by economic and political means in the face of threats to the NATO organization collectively and NATO nations individually.

It would be difficult to attempt to formulate a pattern for success among the many Negro women who have risen to high offices and places of appointment politically. Each has had to find her own road to arrive at her goal. Some have flashed brilliantly on the scene, then drifted just as quickly into eclipse. Others have remained steadfast, providing leadership and offering proof that the Negro woman has not only found a place in politics but intends to remain there. They may not have achieved all their ends, but their attitude may very well be similar to an opinion once voiced by Edith Sampson: "As a Negro, I found out a long time ago that part of something is better than all of nothing."

Of all Negro politicians, both male and female, probably none ever had a greater association as confidante and advisor to a United States President than did the late Mary McLeod Bethune. During the New Deal Administration of Franklin D. Roosevelt, she was a frequent visitor to the White House and was called upon regularly to confer with and advise the President. So impressed was Roosevelt with her capabilities that he created the office of Minority Affairs of the National Youth Administration and named her as administrator. It was a post that distributed some one hundred thousand dollars yearly to aid Negro education in such schools as Howard University, in Washington, D.C., Fisk University in Nashville, Tennessee, and Atlanta University in Georgia. Her friendship with the Roosevelts began in 1934 at a luncheon Mrs. Eleanor Roosevelt gave in New York for women leaders at the old Roosevelt family house. Mrs. Bethune made reference to the meeting in the April, 1949, edition of *Ebony Magazine* in a story written by her and entitled: *My Secret Talks With FDR*. "I had just returned from a European tour," Mrs. Bethune wrote, "and attended the luncheon as president of the National Association of Colored Women. Mrs. James Roosevelt, Sr., was present at the luncheon and it was there that I first met her. I can still see the twinkle in Mrs. James Roosevelt's eye as she noted the apprehensive glances cast my way by the southern women who had come to the affair. Then she did a remarkable thing. Very deliberately, she took my arm and seated me to the right of Eleanor Roosevelt in the seat of honor! I can remember too, how the faces of the Negro servants lit up with pride when they saw me seated at the center of that imposing gathering of women leaders from all over the United States."

While Mrs. Bethune had had an introduction to the Roosevelt family as early as 1934, it was not until 1935 that she met Franklin Delano Roosevelt. In that year she attended a meeting of the Advisory Committee of the National Youth Administration, which was established to provide job training for unemployed youth and part-time work for needy students. The meeting had been called to review and report on the first year's achievements of the National Youth Administration, and Mrs. Bethune had been asked to deliver a report on minority group activities. She spoke directly to the President, told him that in many parts of the South the fifteen-dollar and twenty-dollar monthly checks the young people were receiving meant real salvation. Her report also explained how her group was working with Works Progress Administration authorities to provide adult education facilities for the parents of many of these young people. "We are bringing life and spirit to these many thousands who for so long have been in darkness," Mrs. Bethune told the President, "I speak, Mr. President, not as Mrs. Bethune, but as the voice of 14,000,000 Americans who seek to achieve full citizenship. We must continue to open doors for these millions."

When she had finished there were tears coursing down President Roosevelt's cheeks. He leaned forward, and stretching his hands across the table, grasped both Mrs. Bethune's hands in his. "Mrs. Bethune," he said, "I am glad I am able to contribute something to help make a better life for your people. I want to assure you that I will continue to do my best for them in every way." There was a momentary quiet about the room. The President, obviously deeply moved by Mrs. Bethune's vivid portrayal of poverty, need and second-class conditions among Negroes, could not contain his tears. The meeting ended shortly thereafter. As Mrs. Bethune left the room, Aubrey Williams, administrator of the National Youth Administration program, placed his hand on her shoulder and said, "Mrs. Bethune, thanks to you, a marvelous impression has been made tonight for the cause we all represent."

Two weeks after that meeting Mrs. Bethune received a letter from the White House, informing her that the President wished to see her. When she arrived in Washington at the office of Aubrey Williams, he received her with a broad smile and the news that President Roosevelt had decided to set up an office of Minority Affairs in the National Youth Administration, and that Mrs. Bethune was to be its administrator. She immediately declined with the explanation that the great pressures of her duties as President of Bethune-Cookman

College in Daytona Beach, Florida, would not permit her to accept the appointment.

"I'm afraid you'll have to do it," Williams insisted. "Do you realize this is the first such post created for a Negro woman in the United States?"

Mrs. Bethune pondered the heavy responsibilities. She realized that it was a high honor being extended her by the President of the United States; she also realized that it would be a tremendous burden when considered along with her many other duties. The decision was not an easy one. In writing of it later, Mrs. Bethune said: "I thought of the splendid job Frances Perkins was doing in the Department of Labor, and Mary Anderson in the Children's Bureau of the same department, and I felt that if these splendid white women were working at such responsible jobs at a time of national crisis I could do the same thing. I visualized dozens of Negro women coming after me, filling positions of high trust and strategic importance. God, I knew, would give me the requisite strength, wisdom and administrative ability to do the job. I told Aubrey I would accept."

For ten years the office of Minority Affairs functioned under Mrs. Bethune's administration, bringing needed benefits to Negro youths across the nation. It served to wipe out race differentials operating in the National Youth Administration and extended training and educational opportunities to Negroes. In Mrs. Bethune's opinion, no government agency did more to stimulate higher education among Negroes than did the Office of Minority Group Affairs of the National Youth Administration.

Though not a politician in the sense that she ever sought elective office, Mrs. Bethune was indeed a politician when measured against the qualifications of enjoying high level political contacts and being looked upon as a spokesman for Negroes.

In her many audiences with President Roosevelt, which were as frequent as seven and eight times a year, the discussions usually revolved around problems concerning Negroes, sometimes with the Chief Executive seeking advice, or at other times with Mrs. Bethune directing his attention to some important matter. Their association was warm and friendly, although on one occasion Mrs. Bethune became so emotionally caught up in the appeal she was making that she embarrassingly found herself shaking her finger in the President's face. It was the time when a Congressional Committee, seeking to effect a sweeping economy program, sought to abolish the one-hundred-thousand-dollar special higher education fund which was dispensed by Mrs. Bethune's National Youth Administration group. Mrs. Bethune arranged a meeting with the President, and after exchanging brief pleasantries, immediately went to the heart of the matter. She reminded the President of the Congressional attempt to abolish the one-hundred-thousand-dollar fund which helped further graduate training of Negroes and told him what a disaster this would be for the potential Negro leaders seeking training in various fields.

"Think what a terrible tragedy it would be for America," she told the President, her right index finger extended toward his face and punctuating every word, "if by this action by a committee of Congress, Negroes would be deprived of the leadership of skilled and trained members of their race!" At this point, Mrs. Bethune realized what she was doing, stopped, and stood staring embarrassingly at her finger which was pointing at the President's nose. "Oh, Mr. President," she apologized, "I did not mean to become so emotional." The President smiled warmly, and said: "I understand thoroughly, Mrs. Bethune. My heart is with you." A week after that meeting Congress voted to continue the full appropriation grant to the National Youth Administration.

In her role as confidante, advisor and friend to President Roosevelt, Mrs. Bethune also came to know and understand his astute political tactics. "FDR taught me much about practical politics," she later admitted, "and how important it is that we understand their meaning if we are to make progress in the political arena. . . . More than once I proposed pretty drastic steps to end the hideous discriminations and second-class citizenship which make the South a blot upon our democracy. But Franklin D. Roosevelt usually demurred, pointing out that a New Reconstruction in the South would have to keep pace with Democratic progress on a national scale. He strove to bring the whole country into a unified understanding of freedom. He tried to hold the whole country together so that the whole might be one. But President Roosevelt did not complete his work. Had he lived I am convinced that he would have launched new, bold offensives against bigotry and Jim Crow everywhere. But it would have been according to *his* plan.

"He would say things that would remain with you for the rest of your life. Thus, one day . . . at a reception in 1940, he beckoned to me and opened up a conversation I shall always remember. 'You know, Mrs. Bethune,' he said, looking out of the window and yet speaking directly to me, 'people like you and me are fighting, and must continue to fight, for the day when a man will be regarded as a man regardless of his race or faith or country. That day will come, but we must pass through perilous times before we realize it, and that's why it's so difficult today because that new idea is being born and many of us flinch from the thought of it. Justice must and will prevail.' "

As a woman in political circles, Mrs. Bethune enjoyed a most unique position, in that she headed a government agency, was invited to White House conferences, and participated in top level politics without once having undergone the rigors of a political campaign. Today's women are, by contrast, a more aggressive group in seeking political office in that they are unafraid to take on a male or female opponent in a battle for political office.

An extraordinary example among them is thirty-nine-year-old Mrs. Vel Phillips of Milwaukee, Wisconsin, who in 1956 became not only the first Negro woman, but the first woman to get elected to the city council in its 110-year history. She achieved what seven other women before her had unsuccessfully tried to do, failing always at the primary level. In 1958, she heaped further political laurels upon herself by defeating Mrs. Marguerite Benson for the post of National Democratic Committeewoman, thus becoming the first Negro woman to attain such a high office.

Councilwoman Vel Phillips belongs to that class of politicians who know when to seize opportunity. When the ward lines were redrawn in Milwaukee in 1955, the reapportionment created the unusual situation of producing a new Second Ward without an incumbent alderman. The councilman who had represented the Second Ward, John J. Fleming, found himself now residing outside the boundaries of his ward, with the realignment placing him in the new Tenth Ward. Thus the new Second Ward with a large Negro population, and no incumbent, was virtually up for grabs for anyone aspiring to political office. Mrs. Phillips quickly surveyed the opportunity and announced her candidacy for the post in October of 1955. She had made only one other previous try for office, that being an unsuccessful bid for a school board post in the spring of 1953.

There were indeed many things in her favor. First of all, she had been born and reared in the community. She was charming and attractive, and at the youthful age of thirty-two had the stamina and endurance to wage a vigorous campaign. In her blossoming career, she already had established a number of "firsts." She had helped finance her education at Howard University by placing first in a nation-wide, Elks sponsored oratorical contest to win a four-year scholarship. In 1951, she became the first Negro woman to earn a law degree at the University of Wisconsin. Soon after graduation, she and her husband, Dale W. Phillips, whom she married in 1948 while in law school, became the first husband and wife attorney team to practice before Milwaukee's federal courts. Both had been prevailed upon to seek public office almost as soon as they began to practice law together, but the husband had dissented, insisting that "someone has to earn our daily bread." When the opportunity presented itself to Vel this time, he not only agreed, but also consented to pay for the campaign.

Although an amateur, Mrs. Phillips had already taken the precaution years before to assure herself a name that would be easily remembered. She legally changed her name from Velvalea to Vel because the original name was "Just too unwieldy." In sparking her own campaign, Mrs. Phillips launched an intensive "get out the vote" drive with workers canvassing in each of the 160 blocks that made up her area. She herself had combed much of the territory as a worker for the League of Women Voters, and had learned first-hand of crowded living conditions, blight, disease and ignorance which affected many in the Second Ward. These conditions were incorporated as topical issues in her campaign from the very beginning. "There is a very definite need," Mrs. Phillips said in launching her bid for office, "for interpretation and crystal-clear thinking in the Second Ward in vital matters such as public housing, slum clearance, urban redevelopment and practical enforcement of the new housing code. I intend to speak on these problems at length in my campaign."

While the Second Ward aldermanic post was a plum ripe for picking, it was not a pushover for candidate Vel Phillips. She managed to hurdle the March primary with Democratic backing, but found herself in a four-way race for the post in the April elections. Her victory on April 3 was hard won by a scant 357 votes, although she bowled over one veteran Negro politician, former assemblyman LeRoy J. Simmons, and two white opponents who staged write-in campaigns. The final balloting gave Mrs. Phillips 1,713 votes; Julian A. Nagel, 1,356; LeRoy J. Simmons, 1,186; and Frank J. Kanauz, 808.

The precedent-shattering win immediately vaulted the young woman lawyer into national publicity, and it was the beginning of a political career that has moved along uninterrupted. "There was a real challenge in running," she said thoughtfully the day after her victory, "since there had never been a woman on the council. Women do bring something to public office that men do not. Certainly they are not thinking of selfish motives and must have a real feeling for the work. I thought, too, I can be of service to my special community, as well as to Milwaukee as a whole. . . . Whether I won or lost, I thought that alerting people to the responsibility of exercising their voting privilege was in itself worthwhile to the community."

As a freshman lawmaker in the city council, Mrs. Phillips moved cautiously at first, keenly aware of her doubly unique role of being a woman—and a Negro. Her eighteen constituents were at a loss as to how to address her at first, and constantly fumbled for the proper word which would allude to her feminine status as well as her aldermanic position. They were finally informed that Mrs. Phillips should be addressed as "Madame Alderman," after the city's research library had flipped through several books of authority including Emily Post's *Handbook of Etiquette.*

Politically, Councilwoman Vel Phillips found the going much easier in her second bid to regain her office in the 1960 elections, this time polling a plurality of nearly one thousand votes over her opponent. The April 5 election of that year gave her a total vote of 2,724 votes against 1,771 for her white opponent, sixty-five-year-old Edwin W. Froemming, a former alderman who moved from the Seventh Ward into the Second in order to contest Mrs. Phillips. It was an easy victory for the incumbent Mrs. Phillips, who by now had managed to take political hurdles in stride.

Oddly enough, Vel Phillips' toughest political fight was not in the contest for a city council seat. In 1958, she found herself embroiled in a factional Democratic slugfest for the post of national committeewoman—an intra-party elective office that gave her the powers of casting a vote for the presidential nominee. Her candidacy, sponsored by labor elements and particularly by Frank Wallick, Milwaukee editor of the *Wisconsin*

CIO News, plunged the Wisconsin state Democratic convention into a furor. A front-running candidate for the office was Mrs. Marguerite Benson, state vice-chairman, who, in her twenty-eight years as a Democratic party worker, had held almost every job available except committeewoman. When it became known that Mrs. Phillips was a candidate for the office, Wisconsin Democrats began to choose sides in a bitter factional battle. The race between the two women—one Negro, the other white—split the Wisconsin state convention squarely down the middle. There were charges of "discrimination in reverse," the consensus of opinion being that it was "just as bad to elect someone because she is a Negro as it would be to defeat her because she is a Negro."

When the balloting was over, Attorney Vel Phillips, with scarcely two years in political office, had routed her opponent by a vote of 597 to 477. It was a headline-making victory, with voices of dissent and praise reflecting on the upset political win.

Among her heartiest well-wishers was Congressman Dawson, himself a national committeeman and vice chairman of the National Democratic Central Committee. He wired her: "Accept my sincere congratulations for your election as national committeewoman, for the state of Wisconsin. I know you will serve your party and your country with distinction." In an "off-the-record" discussion of Mrs. Phillips' victory, Dawson let it be known that her election had come as somewhat of a surprise. "I didn't dream anything would happen like this," Dawson commented. "Yet, in troubled times the United States has grown so big, her (Mrs. Phillips') election is like a breath of fresh air."

Two years later, in 1960, Mrs. Phillips again found herself a candidate to maintain her national committeewomanship. This time there was an absence of the cry of "racism," and she scored an easy win over Mrs. Eleanora Wickstrom, a contestant from the rural area of Walworth, whom she defeated by a vote of 677 to 574. Her re-election assured her a voice and vote in high Democratic party councils for another four years and most significantly—a partial control over patronage jobs.

In the tradition of Negro politicians, Wisconsin's Madame Alderman Vel Phillips has waged her own compaign in Wisconsin—particularly in the Milwaukee City Council—to beat down housing discrimination. That state's legislature, in 1961, refused to pass a bill dealing with outlawing housing bias, the supporters of which conducted their own sit-in campaign at the state capitol in Madison, Wisconsin, and among them was Councilwoman Vel Phillips. The next year, as early as February of 1962, Mrs. Phillips whipped together her own ordinance aimed at removing discrimination in sales and rentals of housing in Milwaukee, but it was scrapped in a committee hearing. "There is no question that there is substantial discrimination in housing against minority groups in Milwaukee," Mrs. Phillips said in proposing the six-page ordinance, then went on to point out that similar ordinances had been passed in New York; Toledo, Ohio; and Pittsburgh, Pennsylvania.

The final upshot of it all was that in April of 1962, the judiciary committee of the city's common council, by a vote of 5 to 0, recommended indefinite postponement of the measure, an action which meant that the ordinance, in effect, was killed. The only consolation was that many of her supporters realized that Milwaukee—as is the case with many other major cities in the United States—must find a way to eliminate its racial bias in housing.

While Mrs. Phillips' rise in politics has been both dramatic and successful, she has not been alone as a Negro woman challenging opponents for public office in cities and states across the nation. Beginning in late 1949, and continuing to the present, Negro women began to earnestly seek posts in city councils and state legislatures, almost always waging their campaigns in the big northern cities. Cleveland, Ohio, pointed the way in 1949 with the election of Attorney Jean Murrell Capers to a seat on the city council. It marked the first time in that city's history that a Negro woman had been so honored. Her victory was the result of determination and persistence, inasmuch as she had tried unsuccessfully on two previous occasions to win a city council seat. In her third try for the post, she enlisted the aid of master campaign strategist, Congressman William L. Dawson, who visited her in Cleveland several times and gave her invaluable pointers on electioneering and precinct organization. Instead of concentrating on placards and advertising as she had done in the past, Attorney Capers now set about building precinct clubs and managed to organize twenty-seven of twenty-nine precincts in the Eleventh Ward, one of Cleveland's largest. She conducted a door-to-door drive, convincing housewives to give her—a woman—a chance to represent them in the city council. She gave market bags to the mothers and bags of candy to the children. In the final campaign stages she drove a sound truck through the ward, and asked the citizens to vote for her. The total result was that she handed her perennial opponent Parker a sound lacing, defeating him by some eight hundred and fifty votes. It was the first time a Democrat had won in the traditionally Republican Eleventh Ward, which held some twenty thousand eligible voters but showed only about a third of them registered to vote. Even more interesting was the fact that Mrs. Capers won without the endorsement of any newspaper, Negro or white, or the support from any labor group. Her career in the Cleveland City Council was a lengthy one, extending over ten years. She is now in the private practice of law.

Negro women apparently have found a seat in the state legislatures a more attractive goal to seek than any other political office. A trend in this direction was started in Detroit in 1950 with the election of thirty-year-old Mrs. Charline White as a representative to the state legislature. She was the first Negro woman to serve in the Michigan Legislature, and though she was described as "a popular member of the House," she was also characterized as "a quiet woman, who seldom made a speech or engaged in debate, and always voted with the

Democratic party." Her career came to an untimely end on September 7, 1959, when she was found dead at her residence, apparently a victim of diabetes and low blood pressure.

In 1952 Michigan again set the pace in electing Negro women to office, this time sending to the State Senate, Detroit Attorney Cora M. Brown. She was the second woman to be elected to the Michigan Senate in its 118-year history. There were several distinctions Miss Brown enjoyed: She was Michigan's first elected woman senator inasmuch as Mrs. Eva McFall Hamilton, the first woman senator, was appointed by the governor to fill the unexpired term of her husband. The other difference, of course, was that Miss Brown was the first woman of her race to achieve the high office.

Her career was in the typical Horatio Alger tradition. She was born April 16, 1914, in Bessemer, Alabama, the only child of Alice and Richard Brown. In 1922 she moved to Detroit with her parents, when her father, a tailor, sought to better his economic opportunities. By the time she prepared to enroll in Fisk University in the fall of 1931, the nation was in the midst of a depression. Her mother took a job as a cook in a private family to help send her daughter through college, and Cora herself worked summers in a Detroit Urban League Camp for underprivileged children to help buy the clothes she needed. There were times, she recalled later, when she had to wear the same dress each day to classes and the same evening gown to all the formals. But she was diligent in her pursuit of an education. Her sociological training led her into a job after graduation with Detroit's Children's Aid Bureau, and later a state job with the Welfare Department. In 1941 she turned her attention toward Detroit's police department and secured a job in the Women's Division. Her contact with Detroit's courts and court procedure generated an interest in the law profession, so she enrolled in Wayne University Law School where she was graduated in 1948.

When politics inevitably beckoned to her in 1950, she lost out in her first try for the Senate by some six hundred votes.

Two years later she ran rough shod over her opponent, Mrs. Geneva McNeal, winning the Third District senatorial post by a vote of eighty-seven thousand to eighteen thousand. At the time of her election, she said: "I don't expect much opposition because I am a woman. I haven't found that too difficult a 'handicap' to overcome. I was surprised and pleased that after I was elected a number of senators wrote me letters saying they were happy that I was going to work with them." Three years later, she was of a different opinion. After completing one term in Michigan's State Senate, she voiced a completely opposite view of her position as a lady lawmaker. She told the *Michigan Chronicle*, in an article published in its December 11, 1958 edition: "I have found sex a greater handicap than ever. And I have talked to many other women who have had the same experience. When I first ran for office, I was told by people in the district there was no place in government for a woman. I think, however, the trend today is definitely away from that. I am still sometimes told there is no place for a woman in government by some of my constituents, but—I hope—they are only being facetious."

Regardless of how she appraised her own position as the lone woman among Michigan's thirty-two senators, she became known as a "champion of the underprivileged." The district which she represented, and upon which she depended for support, was heavily populated with all races and foreign nationality groups, a melting pot of many minorities, whom she aided by waging a fight for community betterment, education, public health, labor causes and civil rights. One of her biggest victories came in February of 1956 when the State Senate passed by a vote of eighteen to eleven a bill which added teeth to Michigan's law against racial discrimination. The measure, co-introduced by Senator Brown and Republican Senator Harry F. Hittle of Lansing, gave the courts power to revoke or suspend all state and local licenses held by business establishments who were guilty of discrimination.

The year 1956 was also a critical one for Senator Brown. In

her vigorous campaign in behalf of minorities and the underprivileged she had, either wittingly or unwittingly, continued to prick at the conscience of Michigan's Democratic party organization. She chose to go a step beyond her post as State Senator to seek the office of Congressional Representative from the First District of Michigan, an ambitious political undertaking, which, if successful, would designate her as the first Negro Congresswoman in history. Her opponent was Congressman Thaddeus Machrowicz, whom Miss Brown accused of neglecting the interest of Negroes in the district while favoring Polish constituents. A showdown contest took place on August 7, 1956, in Detroit, with Senator Brown, lacking support from the Democratic organization, emerging the loser by a vote of 29,663 for the incumbent Machrowicz to only 23,172 for herself.

Two months later, in October of 1956, still smarting from the defeat, Senator Brown further widened her breach with the Democratic party by announcing her support for the reelection of President Eisenhower. She thus joined New York's Congressman Adam Clayton Powell, who had already declared his support for the Republican President, and who had appeared in Detroit earlier to urge Negroes to vote for Eisenhower for the presidency, but vote Democratic on the state and local levels. Like Powell, Miss Brown said she based her decision on opposition to southern supporters of the Democratic presidential candidate, Adlai E. Stevenson. Her announcement of the switch to the Republicans nationally came after a thirty-five-minute conference with President Eisenhower at the White House in Washington, D.C. She was accompanied there by Mrs. Robert L. Vann, publisher of the *Pittsburgh Courier*, a weekly Negro newspaper, which had supported Republican presidential nominees in all elections except 1932 and 1936. When Miss Brown emerged from the White House meeting, she explained at a news conference in the office of then White House Press Secretary James C. Hagerty that she had made her decision on the basis of civil rights. She said she objected to Stevenson's policy of "moderation" on the civil rights question, and added that she believed it was obvious he had "become acceptable to pro-segregationists. I can't conceive," she said, "of anyone being so acceptable to the southern wing of the Democratic party without any kind of commitment or understanding." Of President Eisenhower, she noted that he had "tried in good faith" to implement his civil rights program and had dealt with civil rights with "a larger measure of good faith than Adlai Stevenson."

Back home in Detroit the news was received with headline attention. The *Detroit Free Press* sent its Negro reporter, Collins George, to interview the lady senator and tell its readers why she switched to Eisenhower. The interview, printed in the paper's October 28, 1956, edition, went like this:

"Why did you do it, Cora? When did you make up your mind?"

"It wasn't easy. I said earlier I was going to sit this one out and I meant it at the time. But the more I thought about it, the more I knew I couldn't. I've always told others they should participate in every election, and there I was doing nothing. Everyone knew I had found Stevenson unacceptable as a candidate even before the national convention. Was I just to sit still and let my convictions die by default?"

"You still consider yourself a Democrat?"

"Of course I do," Miss Brown said. "Simply because one faction is in control of the local party machinery doesn't mean that I shall abandon my efforts to make the party truly representative of its name—Democratic."

"Well, Cora, many people say you have killed any chance for a political future for yourself within the Democratic party."

She laughed and said:

"Do you really think I stand any worse with the party now than I did before? The faction in power fought me tooth and nail in the primary. Is there anything more they can do? And if my name is on the ballot under the Democratic label, the people who believe in me will still vote for me."

Her open defiance of Michigan's Democratic party in favor of Eisenhower, brought an end to public office for her in that state. Having relinquished her senatorial post to make a bid for Congress, then defying party leadership to support Eisenhower, she now found herself without political office or favor. Even when she topped a civil service list of eligibles for appointment as a referee in the Court of Probate Judge Nathan J. Kaufman in August of 1957, she saw herself bypassed for the job in favor of Mrs. Jeanne Harbour, whose husband was a turnkey at the county jail. It remained for the Republicans to reward her politically for her efforts in Eisenhower's behalf. On August 15, 1957, Postmaster General Arthur E. Summerfield appointed her to the fifteen-thousand-dollar-a-year post of Special Associate General Counsel of the United States Post Office Department. She was named to succeed the late Attorney Joseph Birch, who died earlier that year, and the new position made a first for a Negro woman on the post office's legal staff. Her tenure in office was terminated when the Democrats regained the White House in 1960 with the election of President John Fitzgerald Kennedy. She has since switched her residency to Los Angeles and returned to private law practice.

New York, in 1954, added that state's name to the list of those who sent a Negro woman to the state legislature as "the first" in history. The honor went to Mrs. Bessie A. Buchanan, a pretty, diminutive, one-time show girl, who, with Tammany Hall backing, won an overwhelming victory for the State Assembly. She was virtually a political novice at the time, her only experience being in the senatorial campaign of New York Governor Herbert H. Lehman—and this at the suggestion of the late Mrs. Mary McLeod Bethune, who prodded her into helping Lehman get elected. Her good looks and rich background in show business were natural accoutrements to help her push through legislative measures in the behalf of New York's Negroes. Almost as soon as she was seated, she submitted three bills in the legislature, headquartered at the capitol in Albany, New York, which sought to strengthen the state's anti-discrimination laws. The measures were co-sponsored by Democratic State Senator Joseph Zaretzki, and provided for the following: 1) forbid insurance companies to discriminate against Negroes in issuing automobile policies and selling fire insurance for real estate; 2) forbid Jim Crow in private-owned housing; and 3) permit the state commissioner of education to enforce a law which provided that state institutions teaching white supremacy be stripped of their charters. The importance of the bills was noted in a *New York Daily News* article of January 17, 1955, which quoted the co-sponsors as saying that "it is difficult, almost impossible for Negro brokers to get auto liability insurance for their clients, even at premiums at least fifty per cent higher than for other car owners." On the matter of fire insurance, Mrs. Buchanan and Zaretzki charged that the insurance companies "simply have proscribed the entire Harlem area by literally drawing a red line around it." "Regardless of condition of the properties sought to be insured," they pointed out, "the insurance companies will not step within that line."

In her successful eight-year tenure of office Assemblywoman Bessie Buchanan became the darling of New York's legislature. When she announced in May, 1962, that she would not be a candidate for re-election, the *New York Herald Tribune* had this comment to make in Tom O'Hara's column in the May 27 edition: "Both Republican and Democratic lawmakers in Albany will be a little sad to hear that Mrs. Bessie Buchanan, a one-time professional dancer, will not run for re-election as Assemblywoman from Harlem's Twelfth Assembly District. Bessie still looks agile enough to slip into a chorus line. She brought a little cheer to boring sessions of the Assembly. . . . The news came with the announcement that the Twelfth Assembly District Democratic Club endorsed Representative

Adam Powell, Jr., for re-election and that Mark T. Southall, leader of the club, will seek Bessie's post in the Assembly. . . . Mark is active in seeking to break up the narcotic racket in Harlem and speaks openly and often of its horrors."

Assemblywoman Bessie Buchanan's natural charm and bubbling personality helped cast her in the true image of a lady politician. It probably came as no surprise then in 1961, when, before a joint session of the Assembly and Senate, Mrs. Buchanan submitted for adoption a new official state song for which she had written the words and music. The catchy, march-time tune was wildly received by her fellow legislators, and when the society orchestra of Meyer Davis and the interracial Malcolm Dodds quartet finished rendering it for the crowded gathering, both Republicans and Democrats rushed to congratulate the assemblywoman. It was indeed a precedent in that Mrs. Buchanan was the first and only legislator ever to enter a composition to be chosen as the state's official song.

In 1958 more Negro women made bids for legislature seats than ever before at any one time. There were four candidates in three widely separated states across the nation. They were Mrs. Thelma C. Evans, a hotel owner in Phoenix, Arizona; Mrs. Verda Welcome, Baltimore, Maryland, housewife and schoolteacher; Mrs. Irma Dixon, a dress shop proprietor and former schoolteacher in Baltimore; and Mrs. Floy Clements, a Chicago, Illinois, widow, who had campaigned vigorously for Democrats since 1927. Three were elected to office. Mrs. Evans, a resident of Phoenix since 1945 and a staunch civic worker, hoped to further legislation to better conditions for minority groups in Arizona, but was unable to gain the nomination in the Democratic primary. On the other hand, Mrs. Welcome and Mrs. Dixon became involved in a heated political contest that saw both emerge winners as Maryland Democrats, but with each having different backing. Mrs. Welcome, as a maverick Democrat, waged an uphill struggle against Baltimore's powerful Democratic machine organization as one among seven on an all-Negro, bi-partisan coalition ticket. Mrs.

Dixon, by contrast, had the blessings of the regular Democratic organization and refused to participate in, or accept, the support of the all-Negro slate. Mrs. Welcome had demonstrated in the Democratic primary of that year that she could successfully challenge the machine organization, headed by businessman James H. Pollack, who has been described as the most powerful political leader in Baltimore. In that May, 1958, primary Mrs. Welcome defeated Arlington Phillips for a place on the November ballot, a contest in which she was the only Democrat not backed by Pollack.

When the coalition ticket was formed, Mrs. Dixon was chosen as one of their candidates for the six vacancies in the Maryland House of Delegates, although it was known that she had the backing of Pollack. In her public appearances she repudiated support from the coalition faction and referred to the all-Negro ticket as an act of segregation "in its worst form." She made known her views in a public statement in which she wrote:

"I see no sense in all this ill-conceived coalition ticket which violates every principle of Democratic American government that demands the election of only the best qualified candidates regardless of race or color. The coalition leaders have chosen their candidates solely on the basis of color—which in itself is an act of segregation in its worst form."

As the campaign waxed hotter, Mrs. Welcome did what other coalition candidates did not do: she carried her electioneering into the white households in the "upper end" of the Fourth Legislative District. It was a move opposed by many of her advisors, who did not consider it wise or that she would be rewarded for her efforts. But Mrs. Welcome countered that she did not wish to "write off" the white vote, and drove her sound-equipped truck into the white residential areas, even into the block where Pollack lived. In her door-to-door approach, she made a direct appeal in seeking support. Her greeting was like this: "I am Verda Welcome. I am a candidate for state legislature from this district. I am a Democrat. I feel myself a candidate of the entire Fourth District, and when I am elected, I shall represent all the people of the Fourth District." Later she commented that despite misgivings of her advisors she was graciously received in many of the homes, mostly by housewives, and that many asked questions and none turned her down. When election day rolled around on November 4, 1958, the amazing thing was that both women led their respective tickets with the highest number of votes, although Mrs. Welcome was the lone Negro to emerge victorious on the all-Negro slate. She polled 16,141 votes to assure herself of a seat, while Mrs. Dixon tallied 16,810 votes as a regular Pollack-backed Democratic candidate. What was even more surprising was that both women, comparative newcomers to politics, topped four white veteran politicians in the polling. Mrs. Welcome, further enhancing her political laurels, in November, 1962, was elected as the first Negro woman to serve in the Senate of the State of Maryland.

The 1958 election of Chicago's Mrs. Floy Clements to the Illinois State Legislature gave her the honor of being the first Negro woman to sit in the Legislature of the State of Illinois. Her election was viewed by many as a crowning reward for more than thirty years of faithful service as a precinct worker in which she boasted of never having lost her precinct to the GOP. She served one term and then retired from politics.

In New York, Mrs. Constance Baker Motley, veteran lawyer for the NAACP Legal and Educational Defense Fund, had the distinction of being the first Negro woman ever elected to the State Senate. Mrs. Motley, who led the legal battle to integrate the University of Mississippi, won a special election in February, 1964 on the Democratic ticket. She polled 3,555 votes against her Republican opponent's 2,261. The election was held to fill a vacancy created when Senator James L. Watson resigned the 21st Senatorial District seat to take a spot on the New York City Civil Court bench.

Alaska and Hawaii, while farflung geographically, are nonetheless feeling the impact of the Negro woman politician. In

June, 1959, Mrs. Blanche McSmith of Anchorage was appointed by Governor William E. Egan to fill a recently vacated seat and became the first Negro to serve in the legislature of the forty-ninth state.

In Hawaii, young and attractive Helene Hale, niece of United Nations Undersecretary Ralph Bunche, was elected a county chairman on the big island of Hawaii by a 212-vote margin.

Chapter VIII

POLITICIANS vs. PEOPLE

THE veteran politician likes to think of himself as a representative of the people, and therefore a leader. His leadership, however, is often more evident in areas concerned with his own re-election to office and the continuance of his party in power rather than with issues which frequently confront the Negro masses. His concern is with organization and use of the ballot according to his party's dictates, and to avoid, if possible, becoming embroiled in touchy civic matters. Because of this attitude, such organizations as the NAACP and the Urban League became spokesmen for the Negro, often to the discomfort of the Negro politician. In cities like Chicago and New York where machine politics dictate leaders, this discomfort sometimes erupts into volatile verbal exchanges between the Negro politicians and leaders of civil rights groups.

These groups employ their own techniques in calling public attention to problems involving the Negro community, but in many areas they are regarded with just as much disdain by the Negro politician when they apply pressure in raising civic issues as they are by the power structure they are beseeching. These groups feel that they are real leaders of the people, and do not necessarily need or seek the sanction of politicians in their campaign against racial injustices. Thus the Negro politician has frequently adopted an attitude of separation, manifested in the idea that politics is politics and civic leadership is civic leadership.

This has been voiced even more succinctly by Congressman William Dawson, who is quick to explain that politics is the art of organizing a community for the purpose of electing candidates to political office, and not a vehicle for the public expression of grievances. As was discussed in Chapter IV, Dawson came under fire from the Chicago branch of the NAACP in 1955 when he declined to take a more vigorous stand in protesting the slaying of the Chicago youth, Emmett Till. The end result was, as we have pointed out, a NAACP election the following year that saw Dawson's antagonist, NAACP president Willoughby Abner, removed from office. In such matters, Dawson and many of his high level political constituents have formulated a kind of defensive attitude which is expressed in James Q. Wilson's book, *Negro Politics,* and purportedly quotes Dawson:

"These people [civic groups] don't understand what politics is all about. I want to teach people how to organize and elect public officials so that we will have someone in power who can speak for us in the party councils and in government offices where it counts. . . . Talking about all these problems won't get you elected and won't help your cause any when you get in office. . . . These other groups raise a lot of fuss, but when the chips are down they come to me. . . . I won't pick a fight with anyone. . . . But if they understood what politics were all about, they would help us to build this organization rather than criticizing it so much."

It is indeed true that the politician and the political machine have their functions just as civil rights groups, ministers and the church organizations have theirs. Their efforts and ends may, on occasion, coincide, but it is more likely that any inertia to raise issues will come from outside the political arena. The Negro political machine which almost always functions as a machine within the white machine—tends to avoid raising issues, yet realizes that such issues cannot be ignored once raised. Whatever stand is taken usually must be one that avoids risking party disruption and antagonism, yet must be one that would seem to be in line with the wishes of the Negro people. At times, of course, it is politically expedient for the Negro politician to push for special interest legislation when it benefits not only himself, but the Negro community as well. An example is Illinois' Fair Employment Practices bill, enacted in 1961, which was tossed around for nearly fifteen years before State Representative Corneal Davis finally enlisted enough support to secure its passage.

What must be understood here, however, is that Davis has offices in Chicago's Second Ward headquarters building—in fact, an adjacent office to Congressman Dawson—and always had the advice of Dawson before proceeding with any moves that might be contrary to organizational policy. It was therefore "good politics" to press for Fair Employment legislation, and the mere gesture of introducing such a measure year after year in the sessions of legislature demonstrated that Davis was constantly working in behalf of the Negro people. It was also good campaign fodder to help him get re-elected every two years.

Of course, Davis, as a state representative in Springfield, Illinois, has a much freer hand politically than do the Negro councilmen in Chicago. This difference is pointed up at length by James Q. Wilson in his book, *Negro Politics*, which states:

". . . There are two principal areas of political combat in Illinois: the Chicago City Council and the Springfield State Legislature. In the City Council, the mayor and his Democratic party are supreme—the party's decisions are the city's policies . . . In Springfield, the Democrats may or may not control the lower house, depending on the fortune of electoral politics, but they never control the Senate. Here the Democratic party does not enforce its will. This difference means that the kinds of issues which cannot be fought out in the City Council are fought out in Springfield. In Springfield, the party can allow its members the luxury of catering to the demands of their constituents with such special-interest legislation as a strong FEPC law or a school re-districting law without fear that it may be embarrassed by its passage. Such legislature is regularly defeated by the Senate where the Republicans are in the majority.

". . . On most race matters, the Negro politician in Springfield is a free agent. No party clearance is needed to propose any kind of legislative solution to the ills of the Negro people. It is rare for a Negro state representative to receive orders from the Negro boss. In the two most recent sessions, such orders came only twice—in both cases on vital intra-party matters such as redistricting and patronage. The officers of Negro voluntary associations are aware of this and know they can take their favorite bills to the Negro politicians, confident they will be received and sponsored. One militant leader said:

" 'They don't like us, but I can't think of a bill we've given them that they haven't supported . . . I think that deep down inside they think I'm right . . . On most matters they are free agents.'

"In Chicago it is a different matter. Here the Democratic party is on the spot: it must bear the responsibility. Few white aldermen and ward committeemen can be described as liberal on race issues, and few can afford to be. The proceedings of the Chicago City Council are generally undisturbed by the advocacy of race ends. . . ."

As a rule the Negro politician is expected "to speak out" when matters involving race arise. When he does not, the issue might become a cause célèbre, much to his embarrassment. Such was the case in Chicago during the past several years when the community has resorted to school boycotts and picketing because of the adamant position taken by the mayor and the school board under Superintendent Benjamin C. Willis on the issues of segregation, "neighborhood school" policy and classroom conditions.

What will come of the matter must yet remain to be seen. But it is a thorny Chicago problem that has the Negro politician looking to his precincts and hoping that Negro reaction at the polls in upcoming elections will not cause the party to suffer in any way. The target of their wrath—and there has been much strong feeling—is the six Negro aldermen whom some observers dubbed as "the silent six" because of their mild protest in the Board of Education hassle. It is doubtful that they will be put to any great political discomfort, but as one member of their Democratic organization put it: "We expect a little trouble [at election time] because of that school board situation, but I don't think it will be enough to do us any real harm." This Democratic spokesman may have been somewhat prematurely optimistic, for the Dawson organization faced one of the strongest challenges to its political control of the Chicago Negro electorate during the 1964 primary election. At that time community feeling was running strongly against the Negro aldermen who had come out in opposition to the second school boycott. SNCC, CORE and other independent groups combined forces to try to oust Representative William L. Dawson in his bid for renomination to the U. S. Congress. A young Negro mortician, Ahmed A. Rayner, Jr., was the candidate of the recalcitrant forces. Though unsuccessful in their bid to unseat "The Old Man," the power of the establishment was shaken, and the word went out that "the silent six" had best tend to some fast fence patching in the Negro ghetto.

By and large, the different aims, incentives and end of purpose of the various Negro leaders including Negro politicians, are directed toward improvement of the welfare of Negroes. And while they may come to agree on many issues affecting the Negro community, there is often great disagreement among themselves with each in turn accusing the other of benefiting from the Negro's "disadvantages." Where the Negro minister is regarded as sometimes exploiting his captive congregations, he in turn accuses the Negro real estate broker and salesman of "block-busting" or reaping huge sums from panic selling of homes in areas where Negroes begin to move in. Both view the Negro politician as "feeding at the public trough" and maintaining his position by doing little or nothing about the segregated wards which help keep him in office. Similar attitudes are held toward the Negro schoolteacher, who, in the main, must depend upon a segregated school—and this despite the Supreme Court ruling against segregated schools—for a job in the teaching profession. This is supported by the pattern in Chicago, and in many other cities, where Negro teachers are principally assigned to teach Negro children. Where there are exceptions, the tendency is overwhelmingly in favor of the white teacher teaching Negro children, and seldom for a Negro teacher to teach in an all-white school. The simple conclusion is that the Negro teacher, like the Negro minister, the Negro politician, and almost all others regarded as "Negro leaders" must look first of all for support from the Negro community, which usually is a segregated community.

It is not surprising then that the inter-mixing of their professional backgrounds is usually found in such race relations organizations as the Urban League and NAACP. The Negro politician, though he likes to think of himself as a breed apart from the so-called civic leader, not only infiltrates these organizations but becomes an officer or board member. An example is the Chicago Urban League where Attorney Earl E. Strayhorn, a staunch Democratic party worker in Dawson's Second Ward organization, is one of the League's three vice-presidents. Also on the Board of Directors are Judge Sidney A. Jones, a former city councilman from the Sixth Ward, and Nicholas J. Melas, whose racial background is Greek, but is an ardent and dedicated politician in Alderman Claude Holman's Fourth Ward. This is not to say that they do not have a vital interest in the community as individuals, but it is certain that they are wise politically in seeking active participation in the inner councils of such community organizations.

The divergent professional pursuits of board members and officers of the Urban League, Negro as well as white, are considered healthy for the League's program of improving community race relations. It may not always have one hundred per cent meeting of the minds on issues, but the rule of the majority still helps determine the best course to pursue.

Politically, Urban League Executive Director Edwin C. (Bill) Berry is no stranger to the inner workings of politics and he has used this knowledge to great advantage in coat-tailing Negro and white politicians in an effort to provide more jobs for Negroes. He was once advisor to the Governor of Oregon, where he helped establish the Urban League branch at Portland. It was then described as the "worst city north of the Mason-Dixon line" where Negroes were concerned in terms of jobs and housing. There prevailed an atmosphere of hostility, born of a Negro population boom that had seen a Negro population of only 1,934 before World War II balloon to a fantastic 25,000 after the war. Berry's task was to help relieve the Negro's plight through community education and better understanding, and one he completed so successfully that when he left ten years later for Chicago, Portland had acquired a reputation of being the "nicest" large city in America for Negroes and its Urban League a model organization.

It is little wonder then that men like Bill Berry are apt to be somewhat of a threat to a politician. He has organizational know-how, the ability to reach the people of a community, and a knack for creating jobs and pushing through beneficial legislation. His twenty-five years' experience in the area of race relations makes it appear doubtful that he would exchange this for any political aspirations. But as a man of the people who demonstrates a conscientiousness in solving the ills of a community, he often makes it painfully embarrassing for the politicians when he expresses his opinions on radio and television.

Chapter IX

KEY NEGRO POLITICAL CITIES

WITH continuing patterns of migration, there is a definite trend toward the Negro population outnumbering the white population in America's fifty largest cities in the foreseeable future. The trend has become fact in Washington, D.C., where Negroes in the nation's capital are in a majority of fifty-one per cent over whites. There are, in addition, some fourteen or fifteen major cities across the nation where Negroes could be a political force to be reckoned with, not only by using their numerical strength to get elected to local and state office, but by their power at the polls in national elections.

While we have discussed New York, Chicago and Detroit at length, some mention should be made of several other cities where Negro politicians wield considerable influence. A prime example is Cleveland, Ohio, where more Negroes sit on the city council than in any other city in the nation. There are a total of ten Negro councilmen among the thirty-three in that city, constituting nearly one-third of Cleveland's law-making body. The statistic is not difficult to understand when one considers that Negroes account for 29.2 per cent of the city's total population. Negroes heavily dominate many of the city's wards. Hence, many of the ten Negro councilmen are veterans like Attorney John Kellogg, who has served ten years in office and is rarely in trouble when he seeks re-election.

A similar situation now exists in St. Louis, Missouri, where there are six Negroes on the twenty-eight-member city council, accounting for 16.8 per cent of the city's lawmakers. Here the ward system prevails, and there is a high concentration of Negroes comprising 28.8 per cent of the total population. Surprisingly, only one among the six is an attorney. The others fall into these professional categories: one is a certified public accountant; another is an embalmer and tavern owner; still another is a union official and tavern owner; a fifth is in the maintenance business; and the sixth is a real estate broker. Additionally, St. Louis Negroes have succeeded in electing at large two Negroes to the twelve-member Board of Education.

For obvious reasons the South has not kept pace with the North in placing Negroes in office, but there are notable exceptions which suggest that the political pendulum is swinging more favorably in the southern Negro's direction. In Nashville, Tennessee, for example, with a Negro population totaling 37.9 per cent of the city's 170,874 inhabitants, militant Negro Attorney C. Alexander Looby was elected to the city council in the late 1950's. In Memphis, Tennessee, where Negroes are 37.1 per cent of that city's 497,524 population, George W. Lee has long been the acknowledged Negro political leader with ability to secure jobs and channel political appointments. And, as we pointed out earlier, Louisville, Kentucky, although a borderline southern city, has had Negroes in political office since 1935 on the local as well as state level.

There are no cities, however, which can compare to New

York City where Negro political office-holders are concerned. Besides such elective offices as congressman, borough president, city councilmen and state assemblymen, New York City, with its tremendous Negro population of 1,087,931 (14.7 per cent) has seventeen Negro judges. There are two Supreme Court justices, four city magistrates, one General Sessions judge, six Municipal Court judges, three Domestic Relations Court judges, and one City Court judge. It would seem that in a city where Negroes constitute only 14.7 per cent of the population, this is an over-abundance of Negroes in political office. But when one examines the all-important forty-five electoral votes the state of New York controls [see chart], it is obvious that Negro political strength becomes an important factor and must be catered to. Moreover, when such strength is highly concentrated, as it is in Manhattan's Harlem, it is a formidable political force.

While it is politically true that the city does not necessarily control the state, nor the state the country, it is certain that in presidential elections the huge Negro vote in America's large cities can be a most decisive factor. Former Vice-President Richard Nixon recognized this only too late, and his lament

KEY NEGRO POLITICAL CITIES BASED ON STATE ELECTORAL VOTE

State Elect. Vote	*City*	*Population* *	*Negro Pop.**	*Negro Pct. of Pop.**
45	New York	7,781,984	1,087,931	14.0
32	Philadelphia	2,002,512	529,240	26.4
32	Los Angeles	2,479,015	334,916	13.5
32	San Francisco	740,316	74,383	10.0
27	Chicago	3,550,404	812,637	22.9
25	Cleveland	876,050	250,818	28.6
25	Cincinnati	502,550	108,754	21.6
20	Detroit	1,670,144	482,223	28.9
13	St. Louis	750,026	214,377	28.6
12	Atlanta	487,455	186,464	38.3
11	Memphis	497,524	184,320	37.0
11	Nashville	170,874	64,570	37.8
10	Louisville	390,639	70,075	17.9
9	Baltimore	939,024	326,589	34.8

* Based on U. S. Census (1960) Series PC–1.

after losing the 1960 election was: "I could have become President. I needed only five per cent more votes in the Negro areas. I could have gotten them if I had campaigned harder." His Republican National Chairman, Thruston B. Morton of Kentucky, also realized with grim political hind-sight that the loss of the Negro vote had helped defeat Nixon. In a *United Press International* story of November 9, 1960, Morton was quoted at a news conference as saying Nixon "took only 10 to 12 per cent of the Negro vote, compared to the 26 per cent President Eisenhower attracted." Asked why this was so, the Kentucky Senator said: "We should have done a lot more in that area three months before. I think we had a product to sell and we didn't sell it." Morton then went on to point out in a reference to the Eisenhower Administration's Civil Rights program that the Republicans apparently had "taken too much for granted."

If Nixon had heeded—as did Kennedy—the warnings of Negro leaders that their efforts were falling short in capturing the Negro vote, he might have intensified his campaign in that area. Kennedy did heed—and Kennedy became President. What happened is best reported in a *Chicago Sun-Times* article of October 16, 1960, written by Charles Bartlett. The writer explained that the Negro vote was fluid, indeed pivotal, and that there was apathy toward both candidates arising from the civil rights struggle. Then he went on to say:

". . . Kennedy had achieved a favorable image among the Negroes by the time of the Democratic convention. He had done well, with the help of Franklin Roosevelt, Jr., among Negro voters in the Wisconsin Primary against stiff opposition of Hubert Humphrey. But the image was badly dented by his selection of Lyndon Johnson as a running mate.

"This new sentiment was quickly discernible in the campaign. When Kennedy spoke in Oakland, California, where his audience was expected to be about one-quarter Negro, very few colored people were noticeable in the massive crowd.

"His audience in Los Angeles had the same pale look and

Kennedy dispatched his chief Negro aide, Frank Reeves of Washington, D.C., to learn the trouble. Reeves found quickly that the Negroes were simply apathetic.

"The Democrats' efforts since then have been to rekindle the Democratic loyalties. Reeves maintained there was not time to rebuild Kennedy's image and said the emphasis should be placed upon the party and upon Democrats like Mrs. Roosevelt, Humphrey, and Senator Paul Douglas of Illinois, with established standing. A heavy volume of advertising—the Republicans as much as thirty-five thousand dollars a week—has been launched toward this end in the Negro press.

"Shepard [Marshall], a member of the Philadelphia city council as well as a preacher, has been meeting with groups of ministers in Southern cities to discourage the spread of anti-Catholicism among a Negro population that is 85 per cent Protestant.

"While some Democrats claim the Republicans have been bribing Negro preachers, Shepard reports he has found few involved in preaching against the Catholic Church. Members of one minority, these ministers are not anxious to stir antagonism toward another.

"Shepard and others say that without fanning, the factor of anti-Catholicism will not count for anything in the election because the sentiment does not exist in any strength among the lay Negroes.

"Republican Negro politicians like Val Washington [then a White House aide] believe that Nixon can cut deeply into the Negro vote if a proper effort is made and adequate funds are expended.

"Jackie Robinson, whose last ditch opposition to Kennedy has led him from Humphrey's camp into Nixon's, has given up his column in the *New York Post* for a role in the campaign.

"The Democrats maintain they are holding their own against these factors, in the North at least. They are particularly confident in Philadelphia and Detroit, where party leadership is strong. Chairman Neil Staebler of the Michigan Democratic party reports for instance that Kennedy is running within three percentage points of the party's strength, 91 per cent, among Negroes. The same is true in Philadelphia.

"Neutral observers in Harlem, where the Democratic vote dropped from 78 per cent in 1952 to 66 per cent in 1956, say the trend is still in doubt and that many are talking of not voting.

" 'There's no passion over who wins,' " reports A. Philip Randolph, head of the Sleeping Car Porters' Union.

"The endorsement of Kennedy by Adam Clayton Powell, who backed Eisenhower in 1956, has been accepted as a logical development in the light of Powell's ambition to assume the chairmanship next January of the House Committee on Education and Labor and his resentment at the Republican administration for persisting in his income tax indictment.

"But Powell is still counted influential among less sophisticated figures in Harlem, and his support will ultimately prove helpful to Kennedy.

"The 1960 leaning of the Negro vote is so far less clear than the trend of Negro political leadership, which is passing from the traditional hands of the ministers into those of lawyers and other professional people.

"New personalities with more crusading spirit are pressing to the forefront in a feverish anxiety to assert the political potential of their race.

"The men leading the fight for equality—Martin Luther King, Roy Wilkins, and Clarence Mitchell, Jr. [of the Washington, D.C., NAACP branch]—are staying publicly aloof from the 1960 contest to preserve their statures for the struggles they expect to continue after November 8."

It is uncanny that writer Bartlett should come so close in analyzing the Negro's position and attitude in the 1960 presidential campaign, for possibly at no other time in history had the Negro vote been so indeterminate. Nixon's record on civil rights was reasonably acceptable to Negroes, and his junket to

Africa in 1956 to help celebrate the independence of the new African nation, Ghana, and the inauguration of its premier, Kwame Nkrumah, was laudable in the eyes of Negroes. But Kennedy had a charm and appeal, and a forthright approach in his manner that won over many Negroes. Furthermore, as a U. S. Senator, he had supported such measures as FEPC and had taken occasion to lend moral support to the sit-in demonstrations with this barb: "It is in the American tradition to stand up for one's rights—even if the new way to stand up for one's rights is to sit down."

Even before the campaign had shifted into high gear Kennedy realized that the Negro vote was going to play a vital part in the election. He told the *Minneapolis Tribune* writer Carl T. Rowan soon after his nomination: "I'd be a fool not to consider the Negro vote crucial. We've got to carry the key northern and western states or we're just not going to win . . . All I ask is that people will look at my views, will look at my record, will look at my stand."

What is so important about the Negro vote that Nixon and Kennedy sought? Just this: To get elected either candidate needed a majority of the 537 electoral votes, or 291 votes to be certified as President. There are six states, commonly known as the "Big Six," which control 181 electoral votes. They are New York, California, Pennsylvania, Illinois, Michigan and Ohio. In the largest cities of each of these states there is a preponderance of Negroes whose vote can tip the scales in a national election. They account for the bulk of registered Negro voters in the "Big Six" states, which, in 1960, totaled an impressive 2,862,000. New York had the greatest bloc with 760,000; then followed Illinois with 567,000; and behind it Pennsylvania with 457,000 registered voting Negroes. California had a total of 425,000; Ohio 390,000; and Michigan 340,000. What is more, there were at the time of the 1960 presidential election, some ten million Negroes registered to vote in the United States, according to a census bureau study.

That the Negro vote was crucial had been established in the

1948 presidential election when Harry Truman emerged a surprise winner over New York's Thomas E. Dewey. In that year Truman's margins over Dewey in the Negro sections of Illinois, California and Ohio were overwhelmingly greater than his statewide margins. The result was that Truman captured these states and was returned to the White House. Had the reverse been true, and they had been counted on Dewey's side of the ledger, he would have become President. The strength of this "balance of power" is further seen in a 1956 *Congressional Quarterly* study in which it was pointed out that in twenty-one northern and western states Negroes hold the balance of power in sixty-one Congressional Districts.

It is interesting also to note that this Negro vote can be pivotal in almost any geographic area and has a high percentage of independents. A Gallup Poll of 1960 indicated this with such statistics as these: twenty-three per cent of the nation's Negroes consider themselves Republican; fifty-four per cent are Democrats; and twenty-three per cent identify themselves as Independents. The latter is possibly a reflection of increased education among Negroes which tends toward more sophistication and a professed interest in such things as foreign policy, national defense and national economy—issues which would elevate them above being Negro and label them more as Americans. Of the Negro's shifting vote Gallup made this observation of the 1956 election: "Of all the major groups of the nation's population, the one that shifted most to the Eisenhower-Nixon ticket was the Negro vote." This was borne out in his estimate that Eisenhower got approximately 20 per cent of the Negro vote in 1952, but picked up about 38 per cent in 1956.

Prior to the 1960 election, Carl Rowan pointed up the shifting Negro vote in the *Minneapolis Tribune* of August 14, 1960. He wrote:

". . . A National Association for the Advancement of Colored People (NAACP) survey of Negro precincts in 63 cities indicated that the GOP gain was even higher than Gallup indicated. But the NAACP breakdown indicated something that Nixon knows he cannot afford to ignore: Most of the 1956 shift to the Republicans occurred in the South, and not in the 'Big Six' states.

"For example, in 1952 Eisenhower got 2,134 votes in the precincts of Atlanta compared with 4,764 for Stevenson; in 1956, Eisenhower polled 9,565 to only 1,640 for Stevenson. A similar reversal of the Negro vote occurred in southern urban areas like Memphis and Birmingham.

"Eisenhower's gain was 36.8 per cent in 23 southern cities, but in 40 cities of the North and West his gain was only 9.9 per cent.

"Nevertheless, the GOP carried 22 of these 63 cities [twelve in the south and ten in the north] in 1956 whereas it had carried only two—Leavenworth, Kan., and Zanesville, Ohio—in 1952 . . .

"Henry L. Moon, public relations director of the NAACP [and author of the book, *Balance of Power*], has pointed out that the Negro vote in 1956 was in large measure 'a protest vote' against southern oppression, which explains why the Democratic losses were greatest in the cities closest to these oppressions.

"Moon feels that many Negroes responded to the Republican assertion that 'a vote for Stevenson is a vote for Eastland,' a reference to Sen. James Eastland (D., Miss.), an avid segregationist.

"Negro leaders aligned with neither party also assert that Stevenson encouraged such a protest vote by refusing to speak boldly on civil rights and by visiting Georgia's then Gov. Herman Talmadge and other segregationists in an effort to achieve 'party unity . . .' "

When the 1960 election day of November 8 finally rolled around it brought out the biggest turnout of voters in the nation's history. Some sixty-seven million citizens—about sixty-two per cent of those eligible to vote—went to the polls to cast their ballot, then waited in nervous suspense for the returns. The drama that unfolded as the candidates wavered perilously back and forth with each new return had not been as suspense-filled since 1916 when Charles Evans Hughes, certain that he had won, finally went to bed two days after the election, only to awaken the next morning and discover that he had lost. The dead heat semblance of the result did not change character until 12:33 A.M. on Wednesday after the election when it was announced over television screens that Minnesota, with eleven electoral votes had given Kennedy the needed majority. What still remained in doubt was California, one of the "Big Six," and Nixon's home state where only a few thousand votes separated the contestants although registered Democrats outnumbered Republicans three to two. First results indicated that Kennedy had received 332 electoral votes to 191 for Nixon, with California, Hawaii and Alaska still in doubt, and a difference of only three hundred thousand votes between them out of the some sixty-seven million cast. Later, in California, where they were separated by a scant few thousand, a re-tally gave Nixon the edge and he was able to add the thirty-two electoral votes to his column to give him a total of 223 electoral votes. This, of course, was still shy of the 269 he needed, but he at least had the satisfaction of knowing that he had not been politically humiliated in his own home state.

Thus it was that Kennedy, with only 50.2 per cent of the popular vote against 49.8 for Nixon, took office to bring an end to the third Republican era of this century and begin the third Democratic regime. His gratitude for the Negro vote in the big industrial cities that had helped him hold the all-important edge was expressed in several precedent-breaking appointments. Most widely publicized was his naming of former San Francisco newsman Andrew Hatcher as an aide to White House Press Secretary Pierre Salinger with the title of Associate Press Secretary. The two, Hatcher and Salinger, had worked together for nearly ten years in political campaigns prior to the Kennedy campaign.

A most impressive account of Negro bloc voting is given in Henry Lee Moon's book, *Balance of Power*, published in 1949. Moon writes on page 51:

". . . The Negro voter certainly has been no less hesitant than other citizens to align himself with corrupt political machines in his group interest. Thus in the Democratic primaries in 1946, Negro voters supported the Pendergast machine of Kansas City, Missouri, in a successful effort to retire Representative Roger C. Slaughter. The Missouri representative, as a key member of the House Rules Committee, had been, perhaps, the one person most responsible for the refusal of that committee to submit to the House the bill for a permanent FEPC. He had boasted: 'I sure as hell opposed the bill for a permanent Fair Employment Practices Commission, and I'm proud of the fact that my vote (in the Rules Committee) was what killed it.' The labor movement, through the CIO–PAC, joined in the fight against Slaughter. President Harry S. Truman personally intervened to assure defeat of the man who had held up legislation which the President had expressed a desire to have enacted.

"In the Fifth Congressional District which Slaughter represented there were 21,000 potential Negro voters, constituting approximately 15 per cent of the total vote. In the 1944 general election, Slaughter had been re-elected, with the support of the Pendergast machine, by a margin of 5,193 votes. In view of the strength of the Negro vote in his district, his open hostility to FEPC seemed to indicate that Congressman Slaughter did not care for this vote or that he did not believe colored citizens were intelligent enough to vote in their own interest. In the next election he was defeated by a margin of 2,783, with 7,000 Negro votes cast against him. His vote in the thirty predominantly Negro precincts was negligible. In two of these precincts he received not a single vote, and the highest was 35. This solid Negro vote was the decisive factor in the defeat of Slaughter. In the subsequent general election, the Democratic nominee was defeated by the Republican candidate. Later, charges of fraud in the primary election were made. To the Negro voter, however, the important thing was the retirement from public life of a man who sought to deny them equality of job opportunity, their paramount demand today."

Of course, enactment of FEPC has since come to brighten the job picture for Negroes in many areas, but such issues where the Negro is concerned are not to be glossed over by the politician, particularly where the Negro holds strength of numbers. And more and more, the numbers are increasing, as we have already pointed out. For the moment, the political tide favors the Negro politician in the big cities of the "Big Six" states, but the solid south with its one hundred twenty-seven electoral votes in eleven states must soon face up to the fact that the Negro in his midst can either be a political ally or a foe. Only time, which is swiftly running out in the hour-glass of justice, will determine how the Negro will cast his lot in the big cities of a new political South.

Chapter X

THE CRY FOR LEADERSHIP

WITH the rise of the Negro middle-class in America's large industrial cities has come a greatly accelerated demand for full equality for Negroes in every aspect of their existence. Along with this demand has come an insistent cry for leadership—a leadership that will be steadfast, fearless, unequivocal and unbending in its determination to attain full citizenship rights for Negroes. This has already been made evident in the wave of protest demonstrations staged by today's generation—mostly college students—in the form of freedom rides, sit-ins, stand-ins, and the Council of Federated Organizations [COFO's] Mississippi Summer Project which has been extended to an all-year effort. Participants have shown a defiant willingness to go to jail wherever necessary to obtain the ends they seek and even to give their lives. Their attitude is that

Negro leaders, politicians included, are moving too slowly in their efforts to bring about the social changes necessary to guarantee them a fuller share in democracy.

The one organization that has felt most keenly the competition from these spontaneous student movements has been the NAACP. Their emergence in recent years has aroused some concern and evoked comment by NAACP executive secretary Roy Wilkins. Here is what *Look Magazine* senior editor Ernest Dunbar had to say in an article entitled "*The Negro in America*" in the April 10, 1962, edition:

"The organization that feels these pressures [community impatience with progress] most keenly is perhaps the 53-year-old National Association for the Advancement of Colored People. If you are not one of the NAACP's 371,060 dues-paying members, you, like most of the other 19 million Negroes in America, probably share its goals. Long damned by white Southerners as a 'radical' organization, the NAACP now finds itself under attack by a growing section of Negro opinion, which charges that it is 'moving too slowly,' that it favors court suits over more direct action such as sit-ins and that it is dominated by middle-class intellectuals who are out of touch with Negro masses and youth. Moreover, its civil-rights preserve is being encroached upon by groups such as the Congress of Racial Equality [CORE], Student Nonviolent Coordinating Committee [SNCC] and the Rev. Martin Luther King's Southern Christian Leadership Conference.

"Roy Wilkins, the Association's Minnesota-reared executive secretary denies this. 'The general proposition that the NAACP has law books under one arm and the Supreme Court under the other is a myth,' he'll tell you. 'Sit-ins? We had sit-ins as long ago as 1929!'

"While giving the student protest groups credit for some gains, Wilkins maintains, 'The youth bring the fire and the drive that's necessary, but it is the adults who do most of the organizing, planning and financing that are the backbone of this fight.'

"Wilkins says those who accuse the NAACP of being 'legalistic' are often those who want to act non-legally! He argues that the groundwork for the Negro's present advancement, including the right to unsegregated interstate travel, was laid by the NAACP in its many court battles . . .

". . . 'I have infinite good faith in the good sense of the American Negro,' Wilkins adds. 'He has managed to survive in a society that has erected every bear trap it could, which has hurt him psychologically with constant demeaning, year after year, decade after decade. But, despite job discrimination and other economic disadvantages, he has managed to send his kids to school, to get them an education. He made friends as he went along—he's a hell of a diplomat, you know. He might have made them by a little "Uncle Tom-ing," but he made them, and he survived.'

"Nevertheless, there are many Negroes within the ranks of the NAACP itself who feel that it is not militant enough about combatting the grievances that affect . . . Negroes in . . . day-to-day activities."

What perhaps has inspired Negro youth more than anything else to take up the mantle of leadership is the non-violent movement of the South's Reverend Martin Luther King, Jr. At age twenty-six, after some twenty-odd years of being in school, he completed requirements for his Ph.D. degree from Boston University, then returned in 1954 to his native South to take over the pastorship of the Dexter Avenue Baptist Church in Montgomery, Alabama. It was a move that projected him almost overnight into national prominence as a leader unmatched in stature since the days of Booker T. Washington. He had accepted the pastorate of the Montgomery church, which was located only a short walk from the State Capitol building, in deference to two possible ministerial posts at churches in Massachusetts and New York. The building which stood in the shadows of his church was the same one in which Alabama had voted to secede from the Union, on January 11, 1861, and the same upon whose steps Confederate President Jefferson Davis took his oath of office on February 18, and from whose dome the first Confederate flag, made in Montgomery, was unfurled.

On December 5, 1955, the Negroes of Montgomery, Alabama, demonstrated to themselves—and to the world—that they could stand together under a unified leadership for a common cause. On that morning, Montgomery's Negro population began a near 100 per cent boycott of the city's buses in protest against its segregated seating arrangements, choosing to walk in many instances rather than continue to be humiliated by the Jim Crow practice. It had been touched off by the arrest four days earlier of Mrs. Rosa Parks, a seamstress, who, rather than suffer the indignities any longer of "moving to the rear" of a bus she had boarded, chose to go to jail.

Community reaction was spontaneous. Among the first to arouse action was E. D. Nixon, who headed one of the civic organizations known as the Progressive Democrats, and who posted bond for Mrs. Parks' release from jail. A chain of telephone calls among other community leaders set in motion plans for an organizational meeting to boycott the city's buses. It was not, however, Martin Luther King who presided at that meeting. Neither was it E. D. Nixon, who was unable to be present as he had to leave Montgomery the day of the planned meeting on his regular railroad run. The man chosen to preside was the Reverend L. Roy Bennett, president of the Interdenominational Ministerial Alliance. The Reverend Dr. King was not elected to head the movement until the night of the first mass meeting on the day Mrs. Parks went to trial and the bus boycott began. But he was elected unanimously to fill this role that eventually marked him as a symbol of new Negro leadership, expressed without violence and dedicated to its principles. Of his election and the leadership that was thrust upon him, the Reverend Dr. King later made this comment in his book, *Stride Toward Freedom:* "The action had caught me unawares. It had happened so quickly that I did not even have time to think it through. It is probable that if I had, I would have declined the nomination. Just three weeks before, several members of the local chapter of the NAACP had urged me to run for the presidency of that organization, assuring me that I was certain of election. After my wife [Coretta] and I discussed the matter, we agreed that I should not then take on any heavy community responsibilities, since I had so recently finished my dissertation and needed to give more attention to my church work. But on this occasion events had moved too fast."

Under the organizational name of The Montgomery Improvement Association, the 17,500 Negroes who had ridden the city's buses under the Jim Crow system were told: "Be loving enough to absorb evil. If cursed, do not curse back. If pushed, do not push back. If struck, do not strike back, but evidence love and goodwill at all times." It was the influence of the Reverend Dr. King's strong leanings toward the pacifist philosophy of India's late Mahatma Gandhi, which he paraphrases in this fashion: "We will match your capacity to inflict suffering with our capacity to endure suffering. We will meet your physical force with soul force. We will not hate you, but we cannot in all good conscience obey your unjust laws. Do to us what you will and we will still love you. Bomb our homes and threaten our children; send your hooded perpetrators of violence into our communities and drag us out on some wayside road, beating us and leaving us half dead, and we will still love you. But we will soon wear you down by our capacity to suffer. And in winning our freedom we will so appeal to your heart and conscience that we will win you in the process."

How effective the Reverend Dr. King's techniques were in accomplishing the goals of the Montgomery bus boycott has already written a new chapter in the pages of American Negro history. Where the common complaint once was that "Negroes won't stick together," this bromide of generations of brainwashing was dramatically dispelled on December 21, 1955, when Negroes, after 380 days of walking rather than riding buses, ended their crippling boycott. They had, despite home bombings, church bombings, jail sentences and Ku Klux Klan intimidations, achieved their goal of abolishing bus segregation, and in the doing, had found a new dignity and self-respect. From all over the world, acclaim for the leadership of Martin Luther King and the indomitable spirit of the Montgomery bus boycotters was voiced with ringing approval. A modern Moses, seeking freedom for his people, had sprung up in the very cradle of the Confederacy and had brought renewed hope to an oppressed people. The two—the leader and the led—had successfully accomplished what they had set out to do more than a year before, and they had done it within the framework of the Reverend Dr. King's admonitions in the closing words of his first address at the first mass meeting. He had said: "If you will protest courageously, and yet with dignity and Christian love, when the history books are written in future generations, the historians will have to pause and say, 'There lived a great people—a black people—who injected new meaning and dignity into the veins of civilization.' "

The youthful leadership of the Reverend Martin Luther King in the Montgomery bus boycott and in his subsequent efforts in more recent years to strike down segregation barriers in other areas of the South has indeed inspired a new leadership among younger Negroes. Whereas a decade or more ago the spokesmen for the Negro were generally conceded to be such national personalities as Lester Granger, national executive secretary of the Urban League; Asa Philip Randolph, president of the Brotherhood of Sleeping Car Porters; the late Walter White of the NAACP and the late Mary McLeod Bethune, today there is a changing of the guard. There are now newer faces, younger personalities pushing to the forefront to take over the reins of leadership, to help guide the Negro's destiny and they will not be silenced. The National Urban League's new director, Kentucky-born Whitney M. Young, Jr., is a stout supporter of such devices as voter registration drives and has re-vitalized the Urban League's national program.

One of the most amazing examples of this grasp of leadership by Negro youth is twenty-four-year-old Clarence H. Mitchell, III, of Baltimore, Maryland, who, in November, 1962, won a seat in the Maryland House of Delegates. He is without doubt a virtual novice at the game of politics, but he followed the rules of election campaigning, organized a youthful staff of college students, and rang enough doorbells to insure his victory at the polls. His knowledge of issues might have been helped to some degree by the fact that his father is the long-time president of the Washington branch NAACP, but more than this young Mitchell had come to learn of issues first-hand as a sit-inner. What was even more amazing than his victory at such a young age was the fact that he had won out over seasoned politicians, who had regular organization backing in a city long known for its machine politics.

As we have already noted in Chapter VII, Baltimore Negroes have continually sought to over-ride Democratic machine politics in the city's Fourth District where Negro registered voters outnumber whites by almost an eight thousand majority. Their dissatisfaction, prior to 1954, stemmed from such problems as poor housing, unequal job opportunities, discrimination in civil service (admission and promotion), and denial of public accommodations, all linked to the absence of Negro representation in the law-making bodies. A successful effort to remedy this situation came in 1954 when three Negroes, Harry A. Cole, Emory Cole and Truly Hatchett, challenged the Democratic machine organization, headed by James H. Pollack, and won seats in the Maryland legislature. Both Coles were Republican and Hatchett was an independent Democrat.

This seemed to reflect on the lack of adequate Negro leadership in the Fourth District at the time, inasmuch as registration figures as of mid-1958 indicated that Negroes held a majority with 30,049 Negroes registered to vote as against 22,942 for whites. Moreover, Negroes then accounted for about 30 per cent of the city's total population of 982,000. The Pollack Democratic machine tended to minimize these statistics in denying Negroes of the Fourth District political recognition. Because of this the general election of 1958 stirred the Negro leadership in the community into forming an all-Negro, bi-partisan coalition ticket of seven candidates for the state legislature. Among them was one candidate for the state senate, Harry Cole, who had won in 1954, and six nominees for the House of Delegates. Party-wise, they represented five Republicans and two Democrats.

A leader in the formation of this all-Negro slate was Baltimore editor and publisher Carl Murphy of the *Afro-American* weekly newspaper. He was instrumental in bringing together on the campus of Morgan State College in September of 1958 some three hundred Negro delegates from sixty communities to discuss and map strategy for furthering Negro progress both politically and economically. In particular the election in the Fourth District was given considerable attention, and much discussion was devoted to the political advantages of an all-Negro ticket. One of its staunch supporters, the Reverend J. Timothy Boddie, pastor of New Shiloh Baptist Church and director of the Church Crusade for Freedom, felt moved to defend the racial make-up of the coalition ticket, lest it be misunderstood that they harbored improper motives. He told the gathering: "There is nothing else we can do if we are going to match fact and reality. We may be charged with extreme racism for advocating this procedure, but we are justified in doing this as long as our Jewish friends elect Jews, Italians elect Italians, and other racial groups project their own . . . our white friends in these five districts (of Baltimore) draw the color line and elect no colored people to the legislature. They have never elected a colored person in all its history and from all indications, never will."

However well-meaning the intentions of the all-Negro coalition ticket, it was subjected to charges of racism, not only by whites and members of the Pollack organization, but by Negroes as well. The big question most often raised was: "How can they agitate for integration one day and contend for a segregated ticket the next?" Even one of the coalition-backed candidates, Mrs. Irma Dixon, chose to denounce it on the basis of segregation, as we have already pointed out in Chapter VII. Her contention was that representation of all the many elements of the population would not be achieved by the election of a strictly racial ticket. She refused to be a party to the coalition ticket, would not accept its endorsement, and repudiated the all-Negro group in every public appearance.

In answer to the charge of "self-imposed" segregation, the coalition forces insisted that their aims were not to further the ends of segregation, but to bring about greater integration of the state legislature. They sponsored advertisements to explain their ticket and their purpose. One such ad read:

"The coalition ticket is the combination of Democratic and Republican candidates for the election to the General Assembly of Maryland from the Fourth District. There are candidates for the state senate and the house of delegates. The coalition ticket is dedicated and committed to the proposition that uncontrolled service to the people is the first prerequisite for election to any office. It is their purpose, by binding themselves together as a team, to put an end to this political cancer.

"By doing so, we will be able to insure free elections and afford the people representation which puts satisfaction of their needs above all other considerations. This ticket is all colored by accident, in that white nominees refused and still refuse to disown Pollack."

The tenor of this thinking was also voiced by Mrs. Verda Welcome, an independent Democratic candidate on the coalition ticket, who eventually emerged as the only winner among the group. In stating her position, she said:

"Because I am so dedicated to the 'one world' idea and work with so many interracial groups I took care to ascertain if the members of the coalition were moved by any racial prejudice. I am satisfied that there are no anti-white sentiments in the coalition.

"On our 1958 slate only Negroes are carried, because the potential white candidates (like many other persons in the Fourth District) are afraid of the present district leadership and will not make a change until the coalition has demonstrated that it can win without the usual Fourth District backing. Once the present strangle hold is broken, both whites and Negroes will be free to seek representation on merit.

"The present political leadership of the city has no moral right to cry 'race' when it has followed such a racial policy itself. In not a single district has a Negro been slated for office on the high grounds of democracy, altruism, and interracial good-will. Even in the Fourth District, Negroes had to break through as independents in 1954, in order to win half a loaf in 1958. In the Fifth District, with 26 per cent Negroes, it has not occurred to any party leader to sponsor a Negro as candidate for state legislature or city council—even when there was a recent council vacancy.

"Down the years, I have never questioned the ability, capacity, or integrity of white persons to represent me in public office. I believed that when they represented 'all the people' well, they represented me well, too. I hold that Negroes can also represent 'all the people,' including their white constituents. . . ."

The leadership provided by the coalition ticket, though representative of the Negro community, was hardly a match for the seasoned machine tactics of the Pollack organization. The opposition moved swiftly to deprive it of its most experienced and capable campaign manager by attacking Samuel T. Daniels for participating in partisan politics while employed by the state. Daniels, campaign manager for Senator Harry Cole, held the office of executive secretary of the Maryland Commission on Interracial Problems and Relations, but was forced by his agency in mid-October to withdraw from political activity. Pressures had been applied by the Pollack forces, despite the fact that it was customary for city and state employes to participate in political activity, to compel Daniels to resign his political post or face ouster from his state job. He signed a written agreement to remain inactive politically, which had the attendant effect of causing other Negroes to become more cautious and less active in the coalition organization, if they or any members of their families were employed by the city or state.

The coalition was a valiant effort, sparked by community Negro leaders, but it availed little in the way of political gains. The Pollack machine slate won six of the seven positions in the legislature. Mrs. Welcome, who led the coalition ticket with 16,141 votes to gain a seat in the House of Delegates was the only victor. Racially, there was no gain over 1954. Three Negroes had been elected to office that year, and only three were elected to the state legislature in 1958. On November 6, 1958, the day after the election, the *Baltimore Sun* summed up the Fourth District political fight with this editorial comment:

"The results show that the rank and file Negroes of the Fourth District were not prepared to go along with a ticket based primarily on race. The failure of the all-Negro appeal leaves the Pollack machine stronger than ever. Only Mrs. Verda Welcome won an independent place in the district delegation, and her success may inspire the Negro leadership to try a different approach next time."

The *Afro-American* newspaper asked in bold-face letters four inches high, "*WHAT HAPPENED?*" Editor and publisher Carl Murphy later supplied his own version of an answer in a public address. He observed that the coalition organization had made five mistakes and proceeded to list them:

"Mistake No. 1: We failed to recognize by all the signs that this is a Democratic year. All over the nation the Republicans were defeated on November 4.

"Mistake No. 2: We failed to take into account that the Fourth District colored voters had registered nearly three-to-one Democratic.

"Mistake No. 3: Instead of five Republicans and two Democrats, we should have nominated five Democrats and two Republicans.

"Mistake No. 4: Some of our candidates had no money to pay workers and no friends to put up money for them.

"Mistake No. 5: Some of our candidates were hard-working people with neither the time nor the disposition to make public appearances and speeches all over the district, or go from door to door, barber shop to beauty parlor, grocery store to churches, introducing themselves, shaking hands, kissing babies, and asking fellow citizens to vote for them."

In many respects Mr. Murphy was right in his observations, but there were other factors, perhaps, which also contributed to the failure of the coalition effort. There was the belief that the coalition failed to draw within its organization sufficient political leaders at the grass-roots precinct level. The feeling was that such experienced politicos tended to steer clear of any organization propelled mostly by ministers. Their argument was that practical politicians would more readily follow the leadership of another politician, but would be hesitant and skeptical of the leadership of the kind of leader who lives in the so-called "Ivory Tower," and knows nothing of the rank and file masses and probably less of politics.

Other causes of failure tended to point to an under estimation of the strong obligations which can develop over a long period of time between a political machine and its voters, particularly among the lower income groups. There is a breed of loyalty that finds its adhesiveness in the favors that are passed around by the machine, the minor jobs that are given out, the protection it affords for such illegal gambling as the numbers racket, and the "fixes" it can put in when arrests occur. Such functions of a political machine bind the recipients to the organization, and they vote—and influence others to vote—according to the dictates of the machine, race pride and race candidates notwithstanding.

This insistent, restless yearning for new leaders is not only voiced by younger men, and symbolized by the Reverend Martin Luther King, but it is being expressed by those of the older guard who recognize that swiftly changing times must be met with a changing leadership. It is a subject of much concern in almost every major city where the huge populations of Negroes reside, and it has become a thesis for Negro speakers called upon to address banquets and conventions. And their words are being heralded, if not heeded, by a loudly applauding Negro mass.

As an example, consider these excerpts from an address given on June 1, 1962, by George S. Harris, president of the Chicago Metropolitan Mutual Assurance Company, at the twenty-first installation banquet of the Dearborn Real Estate Board, Inc. Among other things, Harris said:

"Permit me to begin by making five rather broad observations:

"1. The future of this great land—the United States of America—will be determined by the future of our great American cities.

"2. The future of our great cities will be determined by the manner in which they solve the race question in their midst.

"3. Largely because of their failure to solve this race question, our great cities are in trouble—deep trouble.

"4. Our great cities will never arrive at effective solutions to the race question until the solution makers, both public and private, respect the unfettered, independent, forthright participation of qualified, dedicated and honest Negro leadership, and . . .

"5. Last but not least, the solution makers will never show this respect until we as Negroes demand it and make it clear, through our willingness to lead, that we intend to participate in every decision that affects us and the general well being of our city. Because this is our city, too. And, if the population experts are correct, a few years from now it's going to be *our* city more than it ever was . . .

"I will concede that we have made many advances on many

fronts, but so has the entire human race; and before we of this generation brag too loudly about our brilliant march from slavery (much to the credit of our forefathers) we must ask ourselves are we, today, continuing that march in cadence with the rest of the nation—yea, with the rest of the world.

"Do our advances appear dramatic only when viewed in isolation and when measured in the context of an era long past?

"Have we assessed our achievements by the measuring rod of past expectations? If so, we have engaged in self delusion. Our progress—our true progress—must be viewed in the light of our *new* capacities, our *new* expectations, our *new* opportunities, our *new* goals, and above all, in the light of *new* demands of this challenging *new* age in which we live. If we would examine our achievements within that overall perspective, I wouldn't be surprised if we discovered that Chicago's present leadership is respected less today than it was fifty years ago, when we were only 2 per cent of the population.

"Call this pessimism if you will. I choose to call it long overdue honesty.

"When I say there is an appalling leadership crisis in Chicago today, I am being honest with myself and I am being honest with you. There is nothing wrong with self-criticism, self-reevaluation. That is what we expect of other people, and we must do the same with ourselves.

"I can but feel, as I walk and ride through the streets of Chicago, as I read the newspapers, as I watch television, as I ponder the decisions being made in high places—decisions that will shape our lives and the lives of our children for decades to come, I can but feel the thunderous impact of 800,000 voices, the voices of my people, crying out for leadership. At times it is a deafening sound. It rings from every slum building, it echoes through the canyons of public housing projects along South State Street. It rings through the bars of the county jail, the detention homes, and I can feel it late at night when gangs of youth—Negro youth—prowl the streets, crying through their laughter and profanity . . . crying for what? Leadership, a leadership that cares, a leadership that they can trust, a leadership that they can respect, a leadership that they can know and feel . . .

"Our tasks in Chicago are obvious. We must engage in a two-fold leadership campaign. We must continue to voice our sentiments before the city's policy makers and at the same time, we must take the cause of democracy to our own people, regardless of their status, regardless of their education, regardless of neighborhood, regardless of religion. We must let them know that we, the privileged, have not deserted them; we must give them the benefit of our knowledge and experiences; we must impart hope and inspiration. We must let them know that they are powerful, that they can become their own Moses. In fact, let's start saying 'we' can become '*our*' own Moses. We must let them know that Chicago is their town, too; that we too can win first class citizenship. And the entire city will be the better because of it.

"If we are partially successful in this great effort, we will also discover what our brothers have discovered in Atlanta, Georgia, the often forgotten fact that there are many, many white Americans who will join us. Some already have joined us. You see, there are many white people who are sick of segregation. Some don't like it on moral grounds and others don't appreciate what it is doing to them. . . ."

While there are many Negroes in America, who realize, as does Chicago's George S. Harris, that there is a scarcity of dedicated Negro leaders, the problem of what to do about it is not one that is easily solved.

Indeed there are many cities across America where Negroes express dissatisfaction with what is offered to them as leadership, and their displeasure is often evidenced in many ways, sometimes at the polls, at other times in public denunciations of community organizations. This leadership may not always function as their followers would have them, but they are there, and the powers that placed them there are still able to exert their strength to replace them whenever necessary.

Unfortunately, the apathy among Los Angeles Negroes which accompanies this division of "leadership" and "followship" expresses itself in many ways. First, there is considerable resentment of those who would organize and lead; secondly, there are efforts to minimize what leadership has been offered in the past by the older, long-time residents; and thirdly, many of the Negroes who have migrated to Los Angeles from such areas as Texas and Louisiana are not quick to take on the habit of exercising their right of franchise. Moreover, there is a great difference of opinion as to a Negro leader and a "leading Negro." In the latter category, Los Angeles has furnished many who fall into this classification by virtue of wealth, business and professional success, or excellence in a chosen career. But the great need still lies in the area of a "Negro leader," and few have been willing or chosen to wear this mantle.

Such failure in Los Angeles among Negroes politically has served only to strengthen the following of such extremist groups as the Black Muslims, who draw their followship largely from among Negroes of the lower income brackets. Yet, the Muslims have become rooted in Los Angeles, providing a leadership for some estimated four thousand Negroes who believe that such a movement will eventually remove their yoke of oppression. They have established a Temple and scattered businesses in the heart of a vast Negro area on Los Angeles "East Side," and draw as many as eight hundred to one thousand persons to their Sunday meetings. Theirs is but one branch of a politico-religious movement, which has a following of an estimated sixty thousand Negroes in sixty cities across the United States, but which has caused American whites considerable discomfort and alarm. In Los Angeles, as in other cities, the Muslims find a voice in one of the community Negro newspapers or else publish and circulate one of their own. The separation ideology the Muslims espouse already is in evidence in the Negro ghettos of America's large cities, and demonstrated to an even greater extent in the all-Negro towns of Mound Bayou, Mississippi; Boley, Oklahoma; and Brooklyn, Illinois. These have been in existence for the better part of a half century or more, but few Negroes tend to migrate to these areas; they seek instead the cities of the large metropolitan centers. Negroes are aware that a disproportionate amount of money has been invested in church property when compared to Negro businesses, but they also realize that the giants of business and industry have exercised such tight controls over finance that such doors are often shut to him. The Muslims then have only borrowed a chapter from the late Marcus Garvey, the British West Indies-born advocate of black nationalism.

The cyclical re-manifestation of this leadership tug-o-war, which was apparent some forty years ago in the instance of Marcus Garvey and now in Elijah Muhammad and his Black Muslims, is not to be taken lightly. Their activities in Los Angeles, as in large Negro communities elsewhere, are merely a reflection of the restlessness, and disdain for leadership, both political and otherwise, that has not fully satisfied the Negro masses. And while many Negroes in high places of leadership disagree with Muhammad's preachments of white hatred, their criticism is largely of the tongue-in-cheek variety. Here is what several Los Angeles civic leaders had to say in the March, 1961, *Los Angeles Mirror* series:

John Buggs, Director of the County Commission on Human Relations: "I am afraid that the Muslims represent a considerable threat to the peace and harmony of the community . . . but it must be remembered that the Muslim voice is NOT the voice of the Negro citizen of Los Angeles. The actions of this fanatical organization could negate all the work that has gone into the improvement of human relations."

Wesley Brazier, Director of the Los Angeles Urban League: "Very few local Negroes have fallen for this foolishness. They have known hate, and they know that it solves nothing, but I fear that the Black Muslims should not be taken lightly. People once laughed at the Austrian house painter when he began his insane rantings—but how many people laugh at Adolf Hitler today?"

Edward Warren, President of the Los Angeles branch NAACP: "I agree that the Muslim brotherhood is a dangerous thing, and that a cure must be found for their sickness—but please remember that this is all a reaction to past actions by the white people. It is just the Ku Klux Klan in reverse. I hope the Muslims' hateful teachings won't cause white men to look with fear and suspicion on all colored men. The whites must learn the lesson that we had to learn when we once feared that maybe every white man we met might be a Ku Klux Klan member.

"The trouble with the wild teachings of Muhammad is that there is just enough truth in them to make it hard for the rest of us to point out all the lies.

"America will have Muhammad as long as she has Faubuses [a reference to Governor Orval Faubus of Arkansas and the Little Rock school integration disturbance], and we will have Muslims as long as white men wear hooded sheets and refuse to accept the Negro as his equal and his friend."

And so as long as the cry for leadership is unheeded, as long as the vacuum remains, groups such as the Black Muslims, and their off-shoots, will find fertile ground for harvest.

And as the Negro becomes more and more a political issue, as disrespect for law, order, and public morals in the name of "states' rights" and "respect for the fundamental meaning of the Constitution" are made synonymous with a denial of Negro civil and political rights, there can be no doubt about the dangers to the two-party system of government as we have known it. The sinister elements that are joined in the right-wing extremist groups, giving both overt and covert backing to the 1964 presidential nominee of the Republican party, threaten the centralized organization that has heretofore kept the disorganized and chaotic anti-Negro fringe in the United States from fusing with the "solid South" and becoming aggressively fascist in the modern political sense. The danger is both clear and present.

So the cry for leadership goes out not only to the Negro community, where it is so profoundly needed, but to the *total* community, the press, the church, the school, labor and business, some of whose members in apathy and closed-eyed fear have placed democracy on the defensive.

Chapter XI

A NEW DAY AND A NEW DEAL

CONSIDERABLE thought has been given to the idea that if the Negro in America is to achieve full freedom, the leadership to bring about that freedom will come largely from the South. Men like the Reverend Martin Luther King, Jr., have demonstrated that this concept is more than a mere notion, and that if the political and social ills of the South are to be corrected, then the correction must be brought about by intelligent white and Negro leadership working hand-in-hand to provide a better community for all. The denial of the ballot to the Negro in many areas of the South has helped perpetuate the notion of white supremacy, but a new day has arrived for the southern Negro and it has brought with it a new deal for the thinking southerners—Negro and white—who realize that the ballot holds the key to their problems.

The change already has made itself evident. Within the decade since the Supreme Court's historic decision of May, 1954, which threw open the doors of all American schools to Negro and white alike, the chainlike reaction has given the Negro a new dignity and a new sense of pride. The idea of getting the Negroes on the voting registration books will ultimately have its payoff in genuine political representation for the southern Negro. His great strength of numbers in the South, which, despite mass migrations following the waves of racial violence in opposition to the Supreme Court decision, still finds the majority of the Negro population in the South with 55 per cent presently living there, according to the 1960 census, compared to 85 per cent previously. This, in addition to the fact that the once rural South has become increasingly urbanized and industrial in its larger cities, has tended to make the southern Negro more keenly aware of his role and responsibility in the total community. Moreover, the action of the federal courts in upholding the Negro's right of franchise in the South has led to an upsurge in voter registration that has given the Negro an even greater balance of power that is causing white politicians to take a closer look at the Negro community. The political tide is swiftly shifting and it favors the Negro voter in the South, who does, on occasion, risk gunfire and death to exercise his constitutional right of voting.

Just what are the effects of this rapidly changing picture? Merely this: the southern Negro is being wooed more and more by white political office-seekers, and is himself aspiring to office, in some instances, for the first time since Reconstruction. In Galveston, Texas, for example, Negro businessman Thomas Deboy Armstrong campaigned for and won a seat on the previously all-white city council in May of 1961, although his majority was only a scant three votes. The fifty-five-year-old businessman-politician recognized the need for Negro representation in city government as early as 1949 when he made a bid for a position on the Galveston School Board and a later abortive attempt for the post of city finance commissioner. He serves without pay on the city council.

Armstrong's election to Galveston's city council is an indication of what will soon take place in greater numbers throughout the South. The most recent figures of Negro registration on a national level indicated prior to the 1960 presidential election that the heaviest upswing among new voters was in the southern states. The census bureau certified this in a *United Press* news release of October, 1960, on the eve of the presidential election. This is what they had to say:

"There will be nearly 10 million Negroes of voting age by election day—mostly in the South.

"They will be part of 107 million civilian Americans meeting state age requirements for the ballot. In most states the voting age is twenty-one. It is eighteen in Georgia and Kentucky, nineteen in Alaska and twenty in Hawaii . . .

"The greatest bloc of Negroes of voting age—3,068,000—is in the South Atlantic states. This area includes Maryland, Virginia, North Carolina, South Carolina, Georgia, Florida, Delaware and West Virginia.

"In Kentucky, Alabama, Tennessee and Mississippi, there are 1,363,000 Negroes of voting age.

"Some 1,421,000 meet age requirements for the ballot in Arkansas, Louisiana, Oklahoma and Texas.

"New York has the greatest bloc of Negro voters of eligible age, 761,000. Then comes Texas with 624,000; Georgia, 613,000; Illinois, 567,000; North Carolina, 547,000; Louisiana, 518,000; and Alabama, 506,000."

It is significant to note that among the states with the greatest Negro voter eligibility totals, only two are situated in the North, whereas five among the group are in the so-called deep South. Registration activity, of course, did not end with the 1960 presidential election, and the number of new Negro voters as a political segment of the South has now reached even more impressive totals as a result of voter education projects.

Gains on the registration books have already made their

political significance felt in elections almost all over the South. The trend began with the 1960 presidential election when the South realized that the end of an era had come after a hundred years; that with both candidates, and both parties taking a stronger stand on civil rights there was nowhere for die-hard Dixie segregationists to go. The day of the white primary and the Democratic party of a Governor Talmadge of Georgia or a Senator Eastland of Mississippi—and former Governor Ross Barnett of the same state—was slowly rolling to the dead end of its course. The Republicans, with Nixon as the helmsman, were steering a course aimed at reaping a southern Negro vote, which by tradition, and by dissatisfaction with discrimination which was almost synonymous with Democratic politicians in the South, could more easily be gathered into the Republican fold. Their thinking was in the right direction, but their genuine politicking apparently did not hold enough promise for the Dixie Negro, who, in many instances, was still struggling for the right to vote. It was apparent in South Carolina, in 1960, when Negro support gave President Kennedy his 9,561 majority over his opponent, Richard Nixon.

More recently, the trend has become an unmistakable reality. Witness this report in the midwest edition of the *Wall Street Journal* of June 12, 1962. The author is Paul Duke, who wrote:

"Here in this long ago capital of the Confederacy, a majority of the 25 candidates for the city council in today's municipal election are openly supporting an anti-discrimination clause recently added to the government charter. The provision is designed to assure Negroes of fair and equal treatment in the hiring of city employes.

"In Memphis, Tenn., college professor Ross Pritchard is vigorously seeking the Democratic nomination for Congress on a platform that includes a civil rights plank. Young Mr. Pritchard, who hopes to sidetrack veteran Representative Clifford Davis, advocates stepped-up Federal Action if local authorities don't move more swiftly to erase racial barriers.

"In Atlanta, Georgia's Republican leaders trumpeted with considerable fanfare a special invitation extended to Negroes to participate in a recent GOP workshop conference. Their aim: To contrast the party's open-door policy with a previous Democratic party at which Negroes were barred.

"These events herald a significant trend slowly spreading in the South. As Negroes by the thousands sign up to vote, their power at the polls is assuming unprecedented importance and white politicians are starting to court the Dixie Negro electorate as never before—quite openly in some cases.

"Politicians' preparation for the day of mass Negro voting is bringing some strange changes, not all of them out in the open. Veteran politicians, who have ridden the racial issue for years, are taking a softer line on segregation and even quietly trying to build Negro machines. Georgia's Senator Herman Talmadge has moved to smooth relations with Negro leaders, and he assures them that his office door is always open. Six southern Senators, including Louisiana's Senator Russell Long, voted for a Constitutional Amendment to abolish the poll tax in 1962.

"While present efforts to court the South's Negro votes often amount to little more than a friendly gesture, they may well be the prelude to an intensive campaign whenever Negro voting becomes really heavy in Dixie. Such a prospect bodes vast political changes for the South in years to come. At the least, the outlook is for a fading away of the segregation issue as more and more candidates cater to Negro demands; at the most, the end could come for the conservative Democratic leadership which has long dominated the South.

". . . Negroes no longer are content just to elect whites. They also are using their growing ballot-box power to gain office for themselves. Though these office-holders are still a tiny minority, Negroes are winning more seats on local governing bodies, school boards, planning commissions and similar units, either through elections or by appointment from white officials. A Negro serves on the North Carolina State

Welfare Board. Six Negroes, the first of their race, won election to the 106-man Birmingham, Alabama, Democratic Executive Committee in 1962. And in Mississippi, there were two Negro candidates for Congress in the Democratic primaries; though defeated, they were the first to try since Reconstruction days.

"Not only do these developments reflect a growing acuity for politics, but they also testify to the success of the Negro voting registration drives now underway across the Southland. While Negroes still represent only 20 per cent of the voting age population in the 11 states, their registration is increasing faster than white registration. More than 100,000 Negroes have been signed up in the last year alone and there are now about 1.5 million on the poll books. The whites, with some 13 million voters, still constitute a top-heavy majority, of course.

"Long-standing barriers devised to discourage Negro voting are beginning to crumble before Uncle Sam's legal offensives. The Justice Department has brought 27 cases designed to enfranchise Negroes under civil rights laws enacted in 1957 and 1960. In Haywood County, Tennessee, where Negroes make up 61 per cent of the population, no Negroes had voted before 1960; now 2,000 are on the rolls. In Bullock County, Alabama, 800 have been signed up since the Justice Department got an injunction . . . to force registration; only five had been registered before then . . ."

On the other hand, while some white politicians are determined to seek the new Negro voter in the South, there are those who are determined that politics in the South remain lily-white. To this end, reacting to the fear that has been engendered by the Negro demand for equality, many whites are rallying to the ultraconservative policies that have been espoused by the new leaders of the Republican party, and virtually reading the Negro out of power in the GOP.

On August 23, 1964, forty-three Negro delegates and alternates, who had been chagrined at the conservative take-over of the Republican party, met in closed sessions in Philadelphia to discuss ways and means of building an effective Negro organization within the framework of the Republican party in an effort to "support politically and financially our friends in the Republican party and . . . to defeat those who have infiltrated the party and seek to drive us out." The spokesman for the group, known as the National Negro Republican Assembly, may be in the position of the farmer who announced to the populace that the barn door was safely locked, after the horse had been stolen.

Understandably, the southern Negro's insistent demand for his right to vote has triggered a wave of violence in the South, more especially in Mississippi and Georgia. Night riding Ku Klux Klansmen have fired shotgun blasts into Negro homes used for voter registration, and Negro churches used for the same purpose have been leveled by fire. Less violent reprisals have led to mass dismissals from jobs, and those Negroes who do register or attempt to register to vote find their names published in the local newspapers. Despite such intimidation, however, the voter registration drives continue and their final effect will eventually mean political upheaval in the South.

Prophetically Paul Duke in his *Wall Street Journal* article wrote:

"A far-reaching by-product of this parade to the polls may be a spread of the two-party system all through the South and a major re-grouping of Dixie's political forces.

"Assuming that southern Negroes cling to their traditional Democratic ties and that Democratic politicians cater increasingly to them, disgruntled conservativies might well flee in droves to the Republican party, which already harvests a sizable vote from conservative southern Democrats in presidential elections. The upshot: A new liberal-controlled Democratic party comprised chiefly of Negroes, blue-collar workers, small farmers and intellectuals; and an enlarged conservative-run Republican party made up of businessmen, white collar workers, larger farmers and descendants of the old southern aristocracy.

" 'The Harry Byrd Democrat is a goner,' despairs a Virginia

conservative Democratic Congressman. 'We're headed into an era when the South will be run by either Tower-type Republicans or Humphrey-type Democrats.' [The Tower he refers to is the conservative young Texan elected in 1961 as his state's first GOP Senator since Reconstruction; the Humphrey is the liberal Minnesotan, an ardent civil rights advocate, who is the Senate Democratic whip and vice-presidential candidate.]

"Generally speaking, the southern Negro vote has traditionally gone to the Democratic candidate for President in the national elections and to the 'least conservative' Democratic candidate in local and state races. Thus, in Alabama's 1962 primary for governor, the 66,000 Negro vote went solid for state Senator Ryan de Graffenried, who firmly proclaimed a belief in segregation and yet was moderate when compared with the outspoken racism of winning candidate George Wallace.

"Though Republican leaders in Georgia, Virginia and a few other states are soliciting Negro support, chances are Democrats will go right on being the big beneficiary. Most Negroes feel a closer kinship with the Democratic party because of its sponsorship of welfare legislation and through inheritance. And as long as Negroes remain at the bottom of the economic scale, they're likely to vote Democratic.

"But the new, more demanding breed of southern Negro voter is looking for a new breed of candidate to support. Instead of lining up behind men whose major qualification is that they soft-pedal the segregation theme, Negroes are searching for candidates who'll stand up for the things they desire—more laws against discrimination, better jobs for their race and increased unemployment compensation. This burgeoning electorate is beginning to encourage southern liberals and moderates to seek office in greater numbers.

"In time, the Negro vote, plus that of union labor forces, could be powerful enough to permit liberal Democratic factions to wrest control from the conservative governors, congressmen and state leaders who hold sway in most of Dixie.

'An alliance between Negroes and labor is only natural because both want a better standard of living,' contends a southern AFL–CIO official.

"Despite the steady increase in Negro registration, only about 28 per cent of those of voting age are registered in the 11 southern states; 56 per cent of eligible whites are signed up. While there have been few reports of voter discrimination in Virginia, Florida, North Carolina and Texas, the National Association for the Advancement of Colored People and other groups complain that arbitrary administration of voting laws and various restrictions still hinder the registration drive in many small towns and rural areas."

As the race issue becomes a hotter one than civilian or military control of atomic weapons, voter registration drives are being stepped up all over the nation with an eye to the polls on November 3rd. In this direct confrontation between those who are "for us and those who are against us," the need for a politically alert and responsible electorate is acute. An Urban League non-partisan drive among Negroes in sixty-eight cities, with the focus on fifteen cities with more than three million Negroes of voting age, began Labor Day of 1964. Director of the project, Sterling Tucker, indicated many of the problems that Negroes have can only be solved through the political process, and the job of getting out the vote can no longer be left to the professional politicians.

It is inevitable that the South's resistance to the Negro's struggle for first-class citizenship must eventually come to a complete end. With education and the ballot, the Negro of today is determined to have his full share of the democracy he has been promised. There is no mistaking that the direction has been pointed, and with the development of younger, more ambitious political and civic leadership, the Negro will continue to pursue the rights guaranteed him under the Constitution. This is the moment of truth. The day for the New Deal has arrived.

Chapter XII

CHANGE, TRAGEDY AND A TEST OF STRENGTH

THE powerful and determined surge of the Negro revolution could not help but thrash into the open those issues of vital concern to America's 19 million Negroes. Civil rights, long denied this restless and discontented minority group, became a burning political issue in 1963 and at once the battle lines were sharply drawn between its supporters and dissenters in the political arena.

The South, with its long history of chain-rattling, intimidation and disfranchisement of Negroes, bristled and stiffened to ward off what seemed certain to be inevitable change. The North, hypocritical in its preachments against segregation and discrimination, finally began to take a more in-depth analysis of its ills and realized that it too was not without guilt.

The Negro, fired with an enthusiasm for "Freedom Now," and overwhelmingly responsive to the leadership of the Reverend Martin Luther King, Jr., acted out his demands for fuller participation in America with dramatic demonstrations in the streets. Birmingham, Alabama, suddenly was projected into the world's news headlines—not as a steel-producing empire—but as an ugly example of discrimination at its worst. Hundreds went to jail in protest, their efforts at peaceful demonstration violently repulsed by the surging fire hoses of city firemen, and the club-swinging police officers of racist Police Commissioner Eugene (Bull) Conner.

When it ended, an intensified voter registration drive, launched immediately by workers under the Reverend Dr. King's Southern Christian Leadership Conference, produced some 2,000 new voters within the short space of six weeks.

President Kennedy took a second long look at the Negro's discontent and reversed his position. Whereas in January of 1963 he felt that sufficient civil rights legislation existed, he went before the nation's television and radio networks in June of that year to make an impassioned and urgent plea for passage of the most sweeping civil rights legislation in America's history.

By now it was clear that the Negro's organized, direct action protests had great appeal for the Negro masses, and its leaders, though not considered politicians as such, had come to have the ear of the White House in matters of vital concern to Negroes. Then, to further dramatize their insistent demands for passage of the President's Civil Rights Bill, the topmost leaders in the civil rights movement joined forces collectively to plan and stage the most ambitious demonstration ever undertaken in the history of the United States.

Their combined efforts resulted in the historic "March on Washington" of August 28, 1963, in which an estimated 250,000 persons gathered in the nation's capital and marched in orderly fashion down Constitution Avenue from the Washington Monument to the Lincoln Memorial. Their gathering, thousands upon thousands strong, and the amazingly well-ordered proceedings commanded the attention of the world's news media. It was an awesome sight. The great swell of humanity stretching the distance from Memorial to Monument, and it was dutifully chronicled by some 1,600 of the world's newsmen and witnessed by an estimated 80 million television viewers.

If their presence in Washington in such unthinkable numbers could not influence a vote one way or another on the Civil Rights Bill, it did at least serve notice on the dissident Senators and Congressmen that many from among this great throng would be doggedly scrutinizing their individual votes on the bill. A negative vote, or otherwise vigorous opposition, could mean the difference between victory or defeat at the polls in the next election.

Here, then, was a reality to be reckoned with. The Civil Rights Movement, which had had its beginnings as organized Negro protest, had now become a potent political force, able to attract, organize and influence followers in more-than-impressive numbers.

With the obvious support, although it was never formally proclaimed, of such a noted Negro leader as Martin Luther King, President Kennedy had won over many Negroes for his positive and unequivocal stand on civil rights. By tacit endorsement from Dr. King and other civil rights leaders, his re-election would draw heavily upon that increased "balance of power" among Negro voters, who, with fewer restrictions, were beginning to become registered by the hundreds and thousands over the Southland.

To be sure, President Kennedy won the admiration of many—Negroes and whites alike—for his liberal views and expressed sympathies with the Negro and his struggle against oppression. At the same time he created many enemies who took strong exception to his administration. The South particularly had been anything but unanimous in supporting him in the 1960 presidential election though considered to be traditionally Democratic. He carried only half of the southern states when he became President, and there was never any doubt that he was most unpopular to the entire southern wing of the Democratic party.

Thus his shocking death, on November 22, 1963, in Dallas, Texas, at the hands of an assassin's bullet, created for Negroes a state of political emergency. They had come to regard John Fitzgerald Kennedy as a friend of their cause in whom they could confidently place their trust. His outrageous murder while riding in a motorcade in an open car through Dallas streets meant more then to Negroes than the grievous and tragic loss of a friend. His death reminded them all too sorrowfully of the hundreds of lynchings of Negroes in America's sordid past, and now that the man who held the highest office in this nation had himself become a victim of murderous hate, it appeared that the Negro's thrust for first-class citizenship was at once in jeopardy.

The big question then was what would Vice-President Lyndon B. Johnson be like in assuming his new role of President. Could he be depended upon to press as sincerely and earnestly for Kennedy's Civil Rights Bill? Would he be as inclined to call in recognized Negro leadership and discuss with them matters vital to Negroes? Or would he, by virtue of the fact that he was from Texas and of the South, attempt to play the delicate game of appeasing the South and at the same time pacify Negroes?

Quickly, Johnson made his position clear. In stepping into President Kennedy's unexpired term he at once pledged himself to carry out the administration and specifically to urge passage of the Civil Rights Bill. Even as the world's international figures were still being received by him as the new President shortly after President Kennedy's last rites, Johnson was calling and meeting with civil rights leaders while they were still in Washington for President Kennedy's funeral. Later meetings at the White House with all gathered in group discussion indicated, at least to the Negro public, that President Johnson was going to follow the late President's line.

There could be no mistaking this in his first address to Congress in January, 1964. The tone of his message emphasized that America held out the promise of freedom and equality to all men, and he strongly urged passage of the upcoming Civil Rights Bill.

Thus civil rights, on the eve of the 1964 presidential election, had become a blazing hot issue with political offices at stake across the United States from even the smallest local post to the very topmost, the presidency itself. The bill, with its strong provisions for putting an end to the denial of the ballot to Negroes, and its public accommodations section outlawing discrimination, would at last give to Negroes some guarantees of full freedom and first-class citizenship. It could not be expected to become law without a bitter fight led by southern objectors and aided by northern dissenters.

This political climate was ideal for the sudden national projection of any stout opponent of the measure, particularly if he had presidential ambitions.

In this case, such a figure emerged in Barry Goldwater, the Republican Senator from Arizona. He had taken a long look at the Republican party leadership soon after Richard Nixon's cliff-hanger loss to John F. Kennedy in 1960 and quietly launched a sustained drive to capture the GOP presidential nomination. By January of 1964, when President Johnson made his position clear on civil rights, Goldwater too was grabbing headlines in a stepped-up bid for the White House. He was definitely a candidate for the GOP nomination, he admitted, and began setting his sights early on important Republican primaries in such states as New Hampshire, Oregon and California.

He believed he could win, and further, he believed there was enough objection to the Civil Rights Bill by southern Democrats and reactionary Republicans to permit him to be acceptable to elements of both parties once he gained the nomination. In desperation, the more liberal forces of the GOP, which once had regarded him only lightly, believing that he could be stopped, now gave grave and serious consideration to his ambitions.

But they had looked too late. Goldwater, reactionary in his views, opposed to civil rights for Negroes and a believer in States' Rights, had taken a long lead and refused to be overtaken. It appeared that he was braked for a time when Ambassador Henry Cabot Lodge defeated him with a write-in victory in the New Hampshire primary. Or, more hopefully, it seemed that he could be stopped by New York Governor Nelson A. Rockefeller who scored a win over him in the Oregon primary, but was soundly rejected in the later, and perhaps more important, California primary.

With the GOP convention only weeks away, Pennsylvania Governor William Scranton, without having entered any primaries, made the most desperate of moves and announced himself as a candidate for the Republican nomination. It was, for all practical purposes, a useless effort. At best he could be credited with winning many sympathies, but not enough delegate votes to make it matter.

By the time the GOP convention began unfolding its patent script in July, 1964, at the Cow Palace in San Francisco, it was clear to the nation that Goldwater was going to become the nominee on the first ballot. He had voted against the Civil Rights Bill when it finally came to a vote in the Senate after more than two months of filibuster, and with such a record he was not acceptable to Negroes. Worse, it was obvious to many of the old-line Negro Republicans that the GOP was no longer concerned about their opinions, their support, or their very presence at the convention for that matter. They were caught up in a dilemma which seemed to offer no solution short of embarrassment.

They numbered only forty-three among the 1,308 delegates and alternates to the convention, and in other years they had exercised a voice, and perhaps exerted an influence in some quarters, but now they were being ignored in the proceedings, treated discourteously, and virtually read out of the party. Their loyalty to the "Grand Old Party" of Lincoln was now being humiliatingly rejected by what had become the conservative party of Goldwater. Negroes present threatened walk-outs, "walk-arounds," and other dramatic expressions of dissatisfaction with Goldwater as the party nominee, but their protests were pitifully feeble against the surging onslaught of the Goldwater bandwagon. At best the Negro GOP conventioneers could only vow to return home and adopt a "do-nothing" policy about Goldwater or campaign against him by organizing locally groups of "Republicans for Lyndon B. Johnson." In either case their standing in the party was certain to be in jeopardy, and if they did otherwise they could be assured that they would not muster any strength among Negroes.

Thus, when Goldwater, as predicted and expected, was pushed over on the first ballot as the GOP standard bearer in the 1964 presidential election, Negroes faced a new and crucial moment in political history. Worse, Alabama's Governor George Wallace had entered presidential primaries in such states as Wisconsin, Maryland and Indiana, and had rolled up votes in impressive numbers. In each case, he viewed the outcome as "victories" for himself, although he invariably was second and third-best in the election. His showing, however, attracted enough attention to indicate that civil rights had become *the* political issue of moment and that there was sufficient opposition to cause the 1964 presidential election to be a critical contest.

If Wallace remained in the picture as a possible southern or Third Party candidate, Goldwater's chances would be weakened. If he withdrew, the South, which previously had given Kennedy only half its votes, now had in Goldwater a candidate which shared its states' rights views and rejected civil rights. The next move then was quite logically expected. Wallace withdrew. Diehard racists, which had organized behind him, quickly shifted their support to Goldwater in open public declarations for the Republican candidate whose party they once hated with a raging passion.

The Negro voter and the Negro politician now stood face to face with the stark reality that party lines had given way to racial lines. The balance of power Negroes had held as block voters for a candidate acceptable to them would now be given its greatest test of strength. The forgotten years of Rutherford B. Hayes, whose ascendency to the presidency by a single vote had plunged the Negro into political eclipse, had now come full cycle. The issue of the Negro enjoying full citizenship rights and political participation which plagued Negroes when Hayes became President in 1871, has now returned again to be tested 83 years later in a political showdown in which the Negro has the greatest and most crucial stake.

Already the attention is focused upon the elections in the South, particularly in areas where Negroes have considerable voting strength and where they are candidates themselves or give support to certain more liberal office seekers. One contest has already given some indication of what may be expected if the outcome of the August 6, 1964 Democratic primary in Tennessee can be taken as any barometer of change. In that contest, Representative Ross Bass, described as "a deep south liberal" and one who voted *for* the Civil Rights Bill, swept over that state's Governor Frank Clement for the Senate seat of the late Estes Kefauver.

Clearly, the determinant then of the Negro's political future lies in the strength of his voter registration numbers and how wisely he puts those numbers to use. He must, for the health of his political potential, not only give solid backing and support to those white candidates who have demonstrated their sympathies to his cause, but also must produce more able and qualified candidates from within his own race. Indeed the time has come when neither the color of a man's skin nor his religion must be a consideration to qualify or disqualify him from public office. Witness, for example, a most unusual 1964 race for judgeship in Atlanta, Georgia, where a Negro attorney, Donald L. Hollowell, dared to oppose incumbent Superior Court Judge Durwood T. Pye for his eight-year term of office. Judge Pye has had a history on the bench of being unsympathetic in civil rights cases and has invoked unusually harsh sentences. Hollowell, on the other hand, has brilliantly defended civil rights cases of both Negro and white, frequently in Judge Pye's court. The outcome of their contest was certain to provide material for interesting analysis later inasmuch as their total vote was drawn principally from Atlanta and Fulton County, Georgia, where Negroes not only constitute two out of every five persons but are roughly one-third of the more than 200,000 registered voters.

It would indeed be tragic, if the year 1964 would result in a backward trend politically for the Negro, who has just begun to flex his muscles as a participant in the total community, local and national. By courage, determination and sacrifice, he has overcome more than three centuries of oppression and second-class citizenship to secure the right to a voice and a vote in his government, and equal opportunity under the law.

The Negro politician must now make the decision to put the qualities of statesmanship and the well-being of his constituency in the forefront, leaving to others the role of petty politicking for short-term gains and personal advancement. In other words, the election of 1964, probably the most crucial for the Negro, since the Hayes-Tilden run-off, will not only demand of the Negro politician that he produce the vote, but it will also demand of the Negro voter that he conscientiously cast his ballot with cold eyed clarity based on the issues and his own survival and the survival of democracy, not as it has been but as it can become.

INDEX